THE SHROUD

THE SHROUD

John Walsh

A STAR BOOK
published by
the Paperback Division of
W. H. Allen & Co. Ltd

A Star Book
Published in 1979
by the Paperback Division of
W. H. Allen & Co. Ltd
A Howard and Wyndham Company
44 Hill Street, London W1X 8LB

First published in Great Britain
by W. H. Allen & Co. Ltd 1964

Printed in Great Britain by
Richard Clay (The Chaucer Press), Ltd.,
Bungay, Suffolk

ISBN 0 352 30367 0

For

DOROTHY

and John, Timothy, Ann and Matthew

Photo Acknowledgements

1, 3, Popperfoto; 2, 10–12, Gamma;
4, Holy Shroud Guild, Esopus, New York;
5–9, Keystone.

CONTENTS

Contents

APPENDIX

PREFACE

During the last six centuries, millions of words have been written about the remarkable cloth preserved at Turin. More recently, most of this writing has dealt with the one basic question: is it the true Shroud of Jesus or a man-made object? Is it—*could* it be—the actual winding sheet of the crucified Christ, bearing an imprint of His body, or is the whole thing a gigantic hoax, a fantastic forgery, of the credulous Middle Ages? Men of learning and renown have lined up on both sides of that compelling query.

Unlike so many other relics of the Passion—the Cross, the Robe, the Crown of Thorns—the Turin relic does not call on tradition for corroboration. It bears its testimony on its surface—testimony that can be examined and investigated. Since the sensational photographic revelation of 1898, this examination has been conducted along a number of different lines: history, anatomy, chemistry, exegesis, legal medicine, photography, art history and textile manufacture, to name the foremost.

But, perhaps surprisingly, this investigation has not been an official concern of the Catholic Church, in whose nominal charge the Shroud reposes. It has advanced almost haphazardly as the fascination of the problem lay firm hold on this man or that. To date, these voluntary scholars have included such disparate personalities as a lawyer-politician who was also a photographer; a young biologist who climbed mountains and painted; an agnostic scientist who believed in the cloth; and a priest-historian who was an implacable foe of spurious relics.

This book is an account of the work of these men in their persistent probing for the Shroud's secret. I have made no attempt to be exhaustive in setting forth the facts, theories, suppositions and wild guesses that have sprung up since the present controversy started. What I have done, I trust, is to tell the story of this astonishing cloth by letting the reader see in action some of the men who have challenged it and who have been challenged by it. Thus, the story of the Turin enigma unfolds on these pages as it actually happened over the last sixty-four years, the most significant period in the relic's history.

The narrative form makes possible a much simpler and more readable approach to what is essentially a highly complex subject. Few things can compare with Shroud study in the use it makes of the totality of human knowledge. Only archaeology, and possibly the detection of crime, come to mind as parallels. As an archaeological problem, in the sheer intellectual excitement it can generate, the Shroud of Turin stands beside Schliemann's quest for Trojan gold and Carter's unearthing of Tutankhamen. And in this realistic age it is surely no irreverence to say that it presents us with a detective story of fabulous proportions.

Beyond all this, of course, the relic soars into the realm of religion, where, if it is authentic, its value becomes immeasurable. Those who believe in it have already named it "The Fifth Gospel," a term that has brought loud cries of protest from the opposition. And yet, if it is authentic, a "fifth" Gospel is just what it is, since it yields more graphic details about Christ's Passion and death than the New Testament and its commentaries combined.

The facts recorded here have always been available in newspapers, books, documents and human memory, but they have been difficult to gather. I have sought them, off and on, for four years, finally visiting Europe in the search. But I have not set them down here in any effort to convince. Indeed, the reader must come to his own conclusion.

Only this much is certain: The Shroud of Turin is either the most awesome and instructive relic of Jesus Christ in existence —showing us in its dark simplicity how He appeared to men— or it is one of the most ingenious, most unbelievably clever, products of the human mind and hand on record. It is one or the other; there is no middle ground.

J.W.

Part One

1

1898: THE CLOTH
IN THE SILVER CASKET

Standing on the broad steps of the cathedral, G. Pucci-Baudana surveyed the Plaza of St. John. Lines of carefully placed wooden barricades cut it into unsymmetrical patterns and entirely blocked off certain streets. At each corner, a white banner marked with the Cross of Jerusalem waved lazily in the slight breeze. Here and there, specially erected arc lights for use at night dangled from thin poles. On either side of the cathedral, first-aid stations and water fountains stood waiting. Directly across from him, on the other side of the plaza, a newly planted bed of flowers gave the only touch of colour to the wide stretches of grey pavement. He was satisfied: the place was ready for the expected million people who would inundate it and the city of Turin during the next eight days. It was the 25th of May, 1898.

Baudana entered the cathedral and took his place among the dignitaries already crowding the pews. Inside the sanctuary gates, in the space usually occupied by the main altar, there was raised a huge, oblong frame of gilded wood. From high above, a graceful sweep of rich red velvet hangings, trimmed with gold and ermine, draped itself around the frame. Fourteen primitive floodlamps, shielded by yellow silk veils, bathed the sanctuary in a subdued, warm light. At this moment the frame was empty.

Promptly at 9:30, a solemn procession started up a long flight of marble steps, led by white-surpliced Palatine clergy. Behind them, impressive in mitre and cope, walked three Archbishops, two Bishops, their black-robed secretaries and four chaplains of the Italian royal household. At the top, the procession entered a large circular chapel, built entirely of black marble. Around the walls were four tombs of white marble, each topped by a heroic statue of the man buried in it. The roof soared in a series of arched tiers into a magnificent cupola.

In the centre of the floor, on a circular platform, stood an unusual altar. It, too, was made of black marble, and was in reality two altars set back to back. Its ornamentation was heavy and profuse but the total effect was one of richness. On a balustrade that ran completely around the platform, cherubim balanced precariously, as if they had landed only for an instant and were about to flutter upwards again. Lamps hung on arms reaching out from the summit of the altar and the structure was surmounted by a golden sunburst, some of whose metallic rays streamed down to a glass-fronted crypt. Behind this glass, sturdy iron bars criss-crossed to form a cage.

At a few minutes before ten, double doors facing the rear altar opened and the Duke of Aosta entered with his retinue.

A tall, striking figure, he was dressed in military uniform, with a sword at his side and his shining helmet couched in his right arm. His left hand held a small bag made of crimson velvet. He knelt at a special prayer stool. There followed princesses in black dresses, white veils and diamond tiaras, duchesses similarly attired, a prince, two more dukes and a solemn-faced, six-year-old who bore the weighty title of Count di Salemi. All the men, including the little Count wore military uniforms with the green sash of St. Maurice across their chests. From another door a delegation of splendidly dressed laymen came in and took its place. At the front altar Mass began.

In the stillness after Mass, a red-robed priest rose, moved slowly towards the Duke of Aosta and stood waiting. Without a word, the Duke held out the velvet bag. The priest carried it to Archbishop Agostino Richelmy, of Turin, who in turn handed it to another waiting prelate. This man, accompanied by four red-robed chaplains, mounted the steps to the rear altar. Opening the velvet bag, he drew out three keys, then cautiously negotiated a small step-ladder until he stood on the altar. Two priests went up with him. Those in the chapel whose positions allowed them to see watched every move.

The glass fronting was removed from the crypt-like section. A key grated as it was pushed into an iron lock; in the saturating silence, the sound was electric. The two doors of the iron cage swung open to the sides, revealing a smaller iron cage. The three keys from the velvet bag were inserted, each in a different lock, and the side of the inner cage swung down. Reaching into the crypt, the two priests grasped a long wooden box, edged it out and laid it on the altar at their feet.

Archbishop Richelmy, eyes shining with expectation, bent over the box and inspected its two seals. Quickly, he broke them. Assistants opened the cover and lifted out a four-foot-long silver casket, its middle bound with a purple ribbon. From the casket, the Archbishop took what appeared to be a thick roll of red silk and held it over his head while facing the Duke of Aosta. Then he turned, still holding it high, so that all in the chapel might see it. Descending the altar, he reverently placed it at one end of a long table and undid three more restraining bands. With extreme care, the roll was turned back, inch by inch. Gradually, there came into view, inside the silk, a yellowish linen material. The red silk, it now could be seen, was merely a backing on this cloth. When the unrolling was completed, and the strip of linen lay at full length, the little group clustered around the table stared at it, wordlessly.

Before them was a long, narrow piece of cloth that had once been white, but now had the tone of old ivory. It was about fourteen feet in length and less than four feet wide. From one end to the other it presented a bewilderingly mottled appearance; a series of large and small patches, darkened areas, discolorations and brownish stains. The gaze of the onlookers immediately went to the stains: though vague and diffused, they gave an irresistible impression of a human body.

On one half the length of the sheet could be dimly seen the front of the body, with head, arms, chest and legs discernible. On the other half, the back of the head and the broad expanse of shoulders tapering down to hips and legs were visible. The figures had no sharp outlines. Yet, somehow, the stains, fading here and darkening there, managed to convey the image of a man. Smears and trickles of a darker hue, like blood, marred the figure in places.

The face was a grotesque thing, mask-like and expression-

less. Owlish white spots indicated the position of the eyes.
The nose was a dark line running down the middle of the face
from arched brows, the mouth a small, dark blob beneath
which stains seemed to form a beard. Separately, another stain
straggled up from the level of the beard, over the head and
down the other side of the face. Long hair.

Archbishop Richelmy and those with him stared at the
cloth, their eyes travelling slowly from end to end. None of
these men had ever seen the cloth before; now they gazed
in dumb awareness. A priest whispered to the Duke of Aosta
and the Duke rose. Hand on sword hilt and helmet still
grasped in his arm, he approached the table. Kneeling, his
back ramrod straight, he bent forward and touched his lips
to the linen. When he rose, others of his retinue followed,
performing the same act. Princess Clotilde, sister of the King,
remained kneeling after kissing the cloth, and bowed almost
to the floor. Tears glistened on her cheeks. Little Count di
Salemi was last, but his eyes barely reached the level of the
table and the Duke of Aosta had to hoist him.

The cloth was now rolled up in its red silk, placed in a
golden urn, and carried in procession into the crowded
cathedral.

Directly in front of the altar supporting the big frame,
another long table had been set up, on which lay a long board.
Assistants began to unroll the cloth on the board. When it
had reached its full length, a look of consternation crossed the
faces of those who stood near: it was longer than the board
and that meant the frame also would be too short. After
hurried consultation, the Archbishop ordered the ends of the
cloth to be folded under before it was affixed to its backing.

It was five minutes past eleven when the long board, with
the linen spread out and securely fastened to it, was lifted up

and placed in the frame. No glass impeded the view. The sight brought an awed murmuring from those who knelt in the semi-darkness beyond the sanctuary lights. The choir ended its chanting, and in the sudden hush a strong voice rang out. A priest standing in the sanctuary solemnly pronounced the order of excommunication against any unauthorized person who dared to touch the cloth. Even if the offence were committed in a rush of excessive piety, he declared, it would not save the offender. In the pulpit, Archbishop Richelmy stood ready to speak.

Stretching out his hand towards the enshrined cloth, he cried: "Behold above this altar the eternal monument to the sufferings of God crucified . . . come to look upon it, ye who adore the sublime beauty of Christianity; see how the ancient prophecy is fulfilled before our gaze. Immense is our good fortune that we have here this Holy Shroud in our possession . . . centuries have passed, the face of the earth has changed, yet the honours rendered to this sacred sheet have never ceased . . . It is, of course, stained with blood . . . it describes His torment . . . it reveals His wounds. Come and gaze; kneel down and pray; let tears stream unchecked from your eyes. Peter and John found this sacred sheet folded carefully inside the empty tomb . . . I declaim that in Thee, Most Sacred Shroud, the greatest of treasures was enclosed . . . for Thou didst enfold the divine Author of our Redemption."

The Archbishop's words, if emotional in tone, were unmistakable in meaning. The strip of linen cloth that had just been raised over the altar of the Cathedral of St. John the Baptist in Turin, Italy on May 25, 1898, was the actual burial shroud that had once been used to cover the bruised, bloody, naked and lifeless body of Jesus Christ.

His sermon finished, the Archbishop descended from the

pulpit, while the choir intoned the *Adoremus*. The cathedral bells began a festive pealing and cannon boomed throughout the city. The twin sounds told listeners far and wide that the Shroud of the Lord was officially on view. For the next eight days, from five in the morning till seven at night, the streets around the cathedral would be clogged with human traffic. Some of these people would be drawn through sheer curiosity. Some, inevitably, would come to scoff. Most would accept the relic for what tradition said it was. In the absence of proof, the mere possibility of such a thing was thrilling . . . awesome. They would stare and pray as had pilgrims before them for centuries.

They had no way of knowing that the long history of the relic was about to enter a new phase. In the brown stains on the cloth lay a staggering secret. The man who would discover it waited impatiently at the door of the cathedral as clergy and royalty filed slowly out.

2

SECONDO PIA:
A MOMENT OF GLORY

The people of Piedmont in northern Italy are a race apart. Hemmed in on three sides by the formidable Alps, they are also separated from their countrymen to the south, but by a more subtle barrier: a difference in temperament. Patience, order and self-control are pre-eminently the qualities of the Piedmontese. Their capital city, Turin, bodies forth these elements of character: wide, clean streets run sensibly at right angles to each other, and a harmony of design makes all the buildings seem kin. Even the grass in the public parks is disciplined, as if each blade had been measured, then snipped with a pair of scissors. There is in Turin none of the chaotic, if charming, disorder of Rome.

Such attributes of heart and mind, however, are not usually fountains of creativity, and in the middle of the nineteenth century the conclusion that Piedmont had contributed nothing important or lasting to Italian art was widely held. One shouldn't bother, it was said, to look for worth-while art in any form, ancient or modern, in Piedmont. Not everyone agreed with this sweeping dismissal, of course. One who didn't was a young man named Secondo Pia.

Born in Asti in 1855 of a well-to-do family, Pia was one of those men who bring with them into the world a deep and instinctive attachment to their native soil. Appropriately, the name he bore was that of the patron saint of Asti, St. Secondo. Before he was twenty, he had spent many long hours wandering through the valleys of Piedmont in search of its art and history. He would stop at a village, inspect the local statuary and architecture, then visit the town hall to delve into yellowed documents. Another day, his tall, thin figure would arrive at the gates of some secluded monastery, notebooks in hand, begging permission to see its frescos and metalwork or for a closer look at the intriguing columns supporting the roof of its chapel.

Possessor of a mind of surprising range, he was fascinated by science as well as art, especially by physics and chemistry. It was sometime in the early 1870's that all these varied interests coalesced and Pia turned, with intense dedication, to the comparatively new wonder of photography. With a camera, he realized, he could record for study and for the delight of future generations the discoveries he was making almost daily.

In 1870 photography was still in a primitive state; it had been scarcely thirty years since Louis Daguerre had revealed its secrets to the world. For the young Pia to set about learning the techniques in Asti was not a simple thing. There were no schools, no teachers, and if there were any professional photographers, they would not willingly divulge skills that might set up a competitor. Pia bought a camera, any manuals he could get his hands on, and proceeded to teach himself. Making his own glass plates at home, by 1876 he was producing excellent pictures.

For a profession, Pia had chosen the law, being admitted to the bar at Turin in 1878. But neither school nor his work as a lawyer interfered with his trips among the mountains and valleys of Piedmont. His spare time always found him on the seat of a buggy, his photographic equipment carefully piled behind him, on his way to some church or half-ruined monument. Only a man dedicated to his task could have compiled the volume of first-class work that Pia did over the next quarter of a century. Often, he worked in the most difficult situations imaginable. When his search took him indoors, the light usually was badly angled and insufficient. He learned to overcome this difficulty by a judicious placing of mirrors to draw in and direct the little light available. Other problems were not always so easily solved: the necessary perspective and distance; the misunderstanding—even outright hostility—of landowners and proprietors. In his studio, he would lovingly develop his large glass plates, framing and mounting the pictures with a tasteful simplicity unusual for his time. It was one of his proudest boasts that he never retouched a negative; the picture showed exactly what the camera had seen and, good or bad, Pia would not add to it.

In company with others like him—Allessandro di Vesme, Ermanno Ferraro, Riccardo Brayda—he succeeded in time in forcing a revision in the critical estimate of Piedmontese art and culture. Piedmont, the experts began to see, had not been a barren backwater during the development of Italian art.

In the 1880's, Pia forsook the law and turned to politics, becoming successively municipal councillor, assessor and mayor of Asti. Between art and politics, honours flowed in on him; he was a member of almost every artistic and historical society of Piedmont. He took part in exhibitions and congresses in Italy and abroad, obtaining ever-growing recognition of his scholarship and his photographic skills. In 1890 he was awarded the Grand Gold Medal at the first Italian Architectural Exposition, the first of many he was to receive. But the honour that would eventually mean the most to him—despite the many hours of anguish it would cause—arrived at his Turin apartment, in the form of an invitation, in the early months of 1898.

This was a year of celebration for Italy. It was the fiftieth anniversary of the *Statuto*, the constitution of Sardinia, on which the laws of the Kingdom of Italy were based. Every city of any size prepared to mark the event with pomp and display. Turin mustered herself for a showing befitting the queen city of Piedmont: she planned an elaborate, year-long celebration involving exhibitions of industry, religion and art. It was inevitable that Secondo Pia would be called on to serve, even if his friend, Baron Antonio Manno, had not been named chairman of the Committee for Sacred Art. The Baron asked Pia to collect specimens of Piedmontese sacred art and supervise their display in Turin. Plans were also made for an exposition of Turin's supreme religious treasure—the linen cloth with the strange markings.

Just when Pia conceived the idea of photographing the Shroud is not certain. According to some, he was the first to suggest it, offering himself as photographer, with the proviso that he would assume all expenses. Others maintain that a Salesian priest, Noguier de Malijay, deserves credit for priority. What is certain is that the idea was received coldly by Umberto I, head of the House of Savoy and King of Italy. His objections were not unreasonable for a time when photography was only beginning to come into popular use. Many other people felt that the remote, scientific reproduction of a photograph was not in keeping with the aura of devotion that should surround so sacred an object. Serious questions, naïve by today's standard, presented themselves: Would any of the spiritual force of the relic inhere in the pictures? Was reverent handling required of every copy of the photo? How was one to view the buying and selling of the picture for profit?

The King's fears inevitably gave way to the arguments of Baron Manno: The work would be done by a dedicated amateur (Pia did not make a living with his camera but in skill he was the equal of any professional); a photograph would furnish an exact record of the relic if it should ever be destroyed; pictures would spread the knowledge of it far and wide, and it was conceivable that they might even throw more light on its origin and history. The Baron's closing shot was unanswerable: With a million people passing near the cloth for eight days, a picture might be made surreptitiously, and could then be dispersed without any control at all.

The task that now faced Pia had its problems. To begin with, he was not to interfere with the regular schedule of the Exposition; that had been set up months before, and with a million people to be shepherded through the cathedral at set times, no changes in the announced order could be made. This provision had a double effect. It restricted the number of attempts he could make, and it prevented him from gaining beforehand an adequate knowledge of the object to be photographed. He had never seen the relic (he was thirteen years old at the last exhibit in 1868) and his first glimpse of it would be in its frame over the main altar. Also, he would

have to work by electric light, since very little daylight penetrated the fifteenth-century cathedral. The use of electric
light for photography was a technique unfamiliar to him, as
it was to most other photographers of the time. Electricity,
in any case, was not dependable; generated by primitive
machinery, it often fluctuated, brightening and dimming
without warning. Another problem was the elevation at
which the cloth would be displayed. He would need a scaffold
or platform big enough to hold himself and his camera. It
would have to be specially constructed and he would need
help in setting it up and dismantling it, since it could not be
left in place. All this would take time.

In order to get some idea of the appearance of the relic's
surface, Pia inquired in Turin for anyone who had seen the
cloth in 1868. He found a number of old men who were glad to
describe it for him, but the result was a collection of vague
and contradictory opinions. Turning to the literature on the
subject, he was equally disappointed by the inconclusive
nature of the descriptions given by the learned. Most of them
were more interested in speculating on the cloth and its
implications than in supplying facts about its physical appearance. Finally he found a book, published over a decade before,
that gave some details.

"On it the Precious Blood and the spices," wrote its
author, Canon Chiuso, "either through a natural process or
supernatural act, left the holy image of the Redeemer of the
world; on it, as this writer had the opportunity to notice carefully at the last solemn exposition of 1868, are outlined the
wounds of the hands and the feet; there still stands out in a
dark reddish colour the wound of His side; the punctures
made by the crown of thorns placed on His head are still
evident; and one can see the outline of the beard and hair of

the Nazarene Man-God; and there is imprinted the full figure of the body of Our Lord."

Since he was unschooled in the use of electric light, Pia began to experiment. His own home—like most of Turin in 1898—had not yet been wired, so he was given the use of some scientific laboratories where electricity had been installed. Repeatedly, he took pictures of objects in daylight and then re-photographed them in the labs under lights. The results he studied diligently night after night, gradually acquiring a profound knowledge of light intensity, exposure times and plate sensitivity. By mid-May he was ready. In the schedule of the Exposition he noted that there were two lulls, when almost all activity in the cathedral would be suspended: the afternoon of opening day on the 25th, and the evening of the 28th. He would make his first try on the 25th.

At the door of the cathedral, Pia watched the tail-end of the procession as it exited behind Archbishop Richelmy. It was a few minutes before noon; the cathedral would close, except for a guard of honour and some privileged worshippers, until three. At that time the unending flow of pilgrims would start. He had little more than two good working hours to set up his platform and camera, arrange his lighting, check all details, expose the plates, and then remove all his apparatus. His darkroom was ready in the sacristy at the rear of the cathedral; he wanted to see the results as soon as possible.

Moving slowly under a burden of wood of assorted lengths and shapes, tools and bolts, Pia's helpers passed through the gates of the altar rail and into the sanctuary where the cloth was exposed. First laying down a set of wooden rails, like a short section of railway track, they began bolting together the scaffolding that had been built days before and then disassembled. When they were finished, a platform, about six by four feet, stood waiting for the camera. The legs, not quite five feet high, terminated in small wheels that allowed the entire structure to move back and forth on the rails. Another, smaller wooden support was placed atop the platform and Pia climbed up behind it. The big camera, made of wood with metal bindings, was handed up and Pia set it carefully on the support; the glass plate it contained measured about twenty by twenty-five inches. The Voigtlander lens stared directly at the centre of the cloth.

Two floodlights, one on either side of the platform, were turned on, throwing a bright glare on the relic. But the current proved unsteady and the lights brightened and dimmed almost every minute. Each globe was fed by its own generator, and immediately, Pia noted that the one on the left was brighter than the one on the right.

In order to get a more even and diffused light, he had provided screens of translucent ground glass. Now he asked his assistants to set them up, on the floodlights, while he placed a thin yellow filter on the lens. A few minutes later, he announced he was ready and, with a silent prayer, he exposed the plate. From his pocket he took a watch. He had decided, as a result of his experiments, to make two exposures, one of fourteen minutes and one of twenty. Now he stood on the platform, behind the big camera, acutely aware of the way the intermittent current pulsed unevenly in the arc lamps. Nothing could be done about that now. He glanced at his watch; nine more minutes and the first plate would be ready. He would expose the second plate while he started the work on the first one in the sacristy darkroom.

The sharp, brittle sound of cracking glass made Pia look up in dismay. The terrific heat from the floodlamps had broken the glass screens, making them unusable. He stood for a moment, then, with a shrug, climbed down from the scaffold. There was no use trying without the screens, and there was no time to get new ones; it was after two and the doors of the cathedral would soon be opened again to the public.

He would have to wait three days for another try. At least, he thought, he had solved some problems, and he could make use of the time to have electricians steady the current in the generators. His next attempt should go smoother. He was only partly right; when his camera was again trained on the shrine, it would be looking at the relic through thick plate glass.

Princess Clotilde, who had wept on kissing the cloth, was disturbed by what she considered the unnecessary exposure of the cloth to contamination and harm. The smoke from the candles and the incense floating in the still air worried her, but her greatest fear was of the electric lamps pouring light and heat on the unprotected relic from all sides. She suggested that plate glass should be fixed in the frame in front of the cloth. Clotilde's feeling for the relic was intense and personal: after the Exposition of 1868, she had been chosen to sew a new backing on it in place of the old, frayed one. She had performed the entire task while kneeling. The glass was applied.

At 9:30 on the evening of the 28th, Pia arrived at the cathedral to find that someone had stolen the sack of bolts stored with the knocked-down scaffolding in the sacristy. With a sigh, he asked his assistants to set up the scaffolding with whatever materials were handy. He noticed that the glass now covering the cloth reflected both the lights and the golden sanctuary ornaments.

By 10:45 the platform was in place, held together mainly

by wire and rope. In order to give the camera a cleaner view, Pia had the platform moved back along the rails to a distance of about twenty-six feet. The two floodlights now gave steady illumination, and new shields of ground glass muted their brilliance. It was 11 P.M. when Pia opened his shutter for the first exposure of fourteen minutes.

After the failure of the 25th he had decided that he would not use the sacristy darkroom, but would work in his apartment, less than five minutes away by carriage. It was nearing midnight when, with his second exposure of twenty minutes completed, he took both plates and hurried home. Behind him, his assistants began dismantling the scaffold.

A small, red light shone feebly in Pia's darkroom as he gingerly placed the large glass plates in a solution of oxalate of iron. When the first vague outlines began to appear under the shimmering liquid, the anxiety left Pia's eyes and the frustrations of the past few days began to lift. At least there was something.

In the dim, red glare, he held the dripping plate up before his eyes. Clearly visible was the upper part of the altar with the huge frame above it containing the relic. But the brown stain-image seemed somehow different from the way it looked on the cloth itself. It had taken on a moulding . . . a depth . . . a definition. Turning the plate on its side, he gazed at the face. What he saw made his hands tremble and the wet plate slipped, almost dropping to the floor. The face, with eyes closed, had become startlingly real.

"Shut up in my darkroom," Pia wrote later, "all intent on my work, I experienced a very strong emotion when, during the development, I saw for the first time the Holy Face appear on the plate, with such clarity that I was dumbfounded by it." All his life Pia was to remember that moment, speaking of it as a great glory. An emotional man under his old-fashioned reserve, his eyes were often wet after relating the details to a spellbound audience. More than once in these talks, he spoke of the "trepidation" that had seized him and made him tremble.

His first reaction to the unexpected sight in the negative, however, had been mixed with uncertainty. What he saw violated all the laws of photography and he knew it.

The stain-image, diffuse and flat on the relic, now stood out like a picture of an actual body, the contours indicated by minute gradations of shading. The face so bizarre when viewed on the cloth, had become a harmonious, recognizable portrait of a bearded man with long hair. Emotions frozen in death emanated from the features; a vast patience, a noble resignation spoke out of the countenance. Even with the eyes shut, the face was suffused by an expression of majesty, impossible to analyse. All this on his *negative* plate!

Pia knew that in any negative there should be only a re-arrangement of lights and shadows and a reversal of position. Light areas should become dark and dark areas light. Left should be right and right, left. The result should have been the usual grotesque caricature of the original that would make good sense only when printed in positive. Instead, here in his negative was a positive portrait as real as any Pia had ever seen.

As he carefully lowered the plate into a fixative bath of hyposulphate of soda, he turned over in his mind the possible answers to the phenomenon. Had there been some kind of rare photographic accident, something never before encountered? Perhaps some strange property of lighting or camera could account for it. But Pia was an expert with a confidence born of a quarter of a century of experience; he had a sure grasp of photographic principle. He soon rejected any explanation but the obvious one: what showed on the negative was exactly what his camera had seen on the cloth. It was still dark on the morning of the 29th when he hastily wrote a short note to Baron Manno to announce the success of his undertaking. He didn't mention the unexpected discovery in this note; that news he would convey personally.

Later that morning, with a positive print made from the negative, he compared the two. There was no longer any doubt. This incredible portrait existed in the stain-image. Although to the naked eye the brownish stains on the relic presented only haphazard outlines, they must, in reality, form a negative, or at least they must possess, in some mysterious way, the qualities of a negative. Thus, when a picture is taken of the cloth, and the negative plate developed, the stain-image is reversed in light values and relative position and shows positive characteristics. Exactly the same process would occur if a picture were taken of a real photographic negative.

As dawn crept through the streets of Turin, Pia sat before the negative and its print, occupied with a sudden, stunning thought. *No human being could have painted this negative that lies hidden in the stains . . . If it was not painted, not made by human hands, then . . .* gazing fixedly, Pia felt a numbing certitude that he was looking on the face of Jesus.

3

MIRACLE OR HOAX
OR ... *WHAT?*

The news, somewhat surprisingly, did not reach the public until fully two weeks later. When it did, it was an excited newspaperman who broke the official silence.

Baron Manno viewed the strange photograph a day or two after receiving Pia's note and was equally impressed and puzzled. It was up to him as committee chairman to choose the next step and he decided on caution. King Umberto and all members of the House of Savoy must first be informed, and no news should be given out, he said, until a thorough analysis by scholars could be completed. In the meantime, the negative would stay with Pia, where it might be seen by qualified persons. At least one Turin newspaper, though, was already in possession of the facts. *Corriere Nazionale* of June 2nd carried a veiled statement: "The photograph is stupendously successful and has an exceptional importance for religion, history and science. But of this we shall speak later." The paper had agreed to sit on the story.

Then began what one writer described as a "true pilgrimage" to the Pia home. It was a glittering pilgrimage, made up of royalty, high-placed ecclesiastics and scholars. The carriages of bishops, dukes, duchesses and princesses became a common sight on the street outside Pia's house. All were ushered into a darkened room, where they beheld the upright negative lighted dramatically from the back. Princess Clotilde was one of the first to arrive, eager to see the wonderful revelation of her beloved relic. There is no record of her reaction to the sight of the noble-looking face, but it could scarcely have been less than her emotional public reactions to the cloth itself. The words of only one of these distinguished visitors are preserved. The paper that reported the incident said he was a well-known archaeologist and painter, but did not give his name. His remark has the ring of spontaneity: "Either this is the authentic Shroud, or it is God who has painted it!"

Another of these early viewers was Marquis Fillipo Crispolti who, although a titled gentleman, often reported on the contemporary scene for Genoa's *Il Cittadino*, under the name of Fuscolino. What Crispolti saw in Pia's apartment made his newspaper blood race and by June 12th he had sent off an article to *Il Cittadino*. It appeared the next day. "The picture" wrote Fuscolino, "makes an indelible impression . . . the long and thin face of Our Lord, the tortured body and the long, thin hands are evident. They are revealed to us after centuries; nobody having seen them since the Ascension into Heaven . . . I do not want to delay a minute in giving this news."

On June 14th, *Corriere Nazionale*, somewhat disgruntled over the unchivalrous enterprise of its colleague, gave out the complete story. "Now that the indiscretion has been made," it said, "there is no further reason to keep secret the details of an event that will soon become of interest to all Christendom . . . The Redeemer, who had miraculously left the imprint of his sufferings and the lines of His body on the funeral linen, reappeared on the glass miraculously outlined, with an amazing fineness of detail. There appeared the noble figure, anatomically elegant, perfect, divinely beautiful; the face still with an expression of ineffable pain and misery. And there appeared the details of the beard, of the hair, the profile, the scars and the imprint of the rope with which the sacred Body had been made secure to the column for flagellation. In short, after nineteen hundred years, during which the world *contemplated* the figure of the Nazarene by the aid of tradition, the photograph of the shroud has now given us a *picture*."

The Vatican's *Osservatore Romano* picked up the story on June 15th, terming the occurrence "A Marvellous Event." With this, the news was official. During the following weeks it echoed throughout the world.

This echo, however, did not produce the unqualified sensation that has since been attributed to it. Many papers simply printed a short account of the facts, or what they thought were facts, without comment and without follow-up. This reserve in secular circles is understandable now, at a distance in time of more than half a century.

To begin with, news of spectacular discoveries concerning the Bible and early Christianity had become rather common. The science of archaeology had been in full flower for fifty

years and had already provided such fascinating items as George
Smith's recovery of the Gilgamesh Epic, an ancient Chaldean
version of the Flood story written in cuneiform. And in the
weeks just prior to Pia's work, readers were discussing two
finds by a Dr. Brueselbach. The first was, supposedly, a contemporary mention of Jesus' entry into Jerusalem in a record
book maintained by a gatekeeper; the second was a small
manuscript fragment of a prayer, said to be written and signed
by Jesus in his own hand. (Both claims were later disproved.)
Thus, in an atmosphere grown accustomed to such things, the
impact of the Turin news was not overwhelming, nor, except
in certain quarters did it last long.

But there were even more particular reasons for this lack
of sustained excitement. A clear understanding of photographic principles, for instance, was not widespread, and
attempts to explain the Pia discovery often ended in a hopeless
mélange of guesswork and erroneous information. For many
people, thousands of miles from Turin, the reports of a mysterious portrait on cloth, spontaneously appearing on a photographic plate, took on the qualities of a miracle. Those who
from habit did not believe in such things simply dismissed it.
Even most of those who accepted the miraculous could only
imagine that the hand of God had intervened at the click of
the camera to produce the image.

Probably the most important reason was the fact that it
was extremely difficult to obtain reproductions of the picture.
There was no widespread dissemination through the news
media of the day. The copyright had been registered in Turin
and reproduction was stricly controlled. A special committee
began handling the requests, at first a trickle and then a flood,
that came in from every Christian denomination. Before long,
it was necessary for the committee to open an office with a

full-time secretary. But the real problem was in the making of the reproductions, mostly enlargements of the face. This work was being done by Secondo Pia and a small staff, working night and day under a rigid operation. All copies carried two official seals: that of the Archbishop, with the words "Seen and approved," and that of the Sacred Art Commission with the inscription "Seen for authenticity." It was a slow, if necessary, process. Initial enthusiasm often died during the long delay between first hearing the frequently garbled news and finally seeing the picture.

Many publications tried to make up for the absence of pictures by using sketches made on the spot or from eye-witness descriptions. The results were horrendous and misleading. It was the very *perfection* of the imprint in the Pia negative—the fineness of detail, the amazing life-likeness of the face—that so forcibly struck the beholder. These things were not evident in the drawings. Between bad sketches and mangled facts, popular world reaction swung from uncritical cries of "miracle!" to a kind of puzzled reserve.

The *New York Evening Journal*, in its Sunday magazine of June 26th, 1898, devoted nearly a full page to the discovery—and managed to include enough untruth and distortion, in both word and picture, to cause hopeless confusion for the American reader. Under a headline that proclaimed "THE MODERN MIRACLE OF CHRIST'S WINDING SHEET WHICH HAS STIRRED UP ALL EUROPE", it quoted some paragraphs from *Osservatore Romano* followed by some highly inaccurate details about the picture and Pia's work, and then launched into a discussion of Veronica's Veil. It was illustrated by the sketches of A. Bianchini, who had been commissioned for the work by the *London Graphic*. Bianchini's depiction of the image on the Shroud was almost incomprehensibly bad. It bore no relation

to the actuality. Most of the world's press similarly emascu-
lated the story.

Baron Manno was soon satisfied that the photograph had
been the result of a natural process. He and others agreed with
Pia that the negative-positive aspect of the discovery proved
the relic's authenticity. On June 19th, the original negative
was placed on public display, again in a darkened room with
special illumination. The Turinese responded in droves.

Inevitably, as the days passed, stronger notes of doubt
crept into published discussions, especially in France and Italy
Some thought the image might have been an accident of
"transparency," meaning that the relic had been photographed out of its frame with the light source coming from
behind. Others suggested "refraction" might account for it,
but no one, it seems, was too sure exactly what that meant.
"Over-exposure" was still another possibility advanced.
More incisive probing appeared in September in the French
Le Moniteur de la Photographie. The magazine had consulted a
Viennese photographer, who replied that he could not give a
valid opinion until he had at least seen the Pia negatives. But,
he ventured:

> All photographers know, no matter how little their
> experience, that negatives of many objects bring out details
> hidden to the naked eye. Such, for instance, is the case in
> the reproduction of parchments, which often clearly
> shows passages that have been effaced or scratched out.
> Therefore it could be concluded that someone could have
> painted on that sheet, a long time ago, the body of Christ
> with the paints of the period and traced the outline with
> some colouring matter, so that in the course of the cen-

turies the paint of the outline has faded and reappeared more distinctly in the photographic reproduction.

Such speculation, it was realized, presented legitimate possibilities. But another objection, slyly subtle, began to insinuate itself among the less scholarly and those emotionally disposed to reject the relic. Pia was accused of deliberate deception. Alone in his darkroom, it was whispered, the photographer had retouched the negative to give it an astoundingly real aspect. He had then made a positive from this retouched negative and re-photographed the positive, ending up with nothing more than a hoax, a forgery. With this process, it was charged, he had been able to deceive all the officials of Turin. (The rumour may have been founded in the fact that Pia, in order to safeguard the original negative, did produce a second negative from the first.)

This rumour would later appear in print, crushing the conscientious Pia, whose respect for his art had always prevented him from retouching even the most inconsequential pictures. A comparison with the relic itself would have killed the vicious accusation, but the cloth lay, silent and inaccessible, in its dark crypt atop the black marble altar. It had been put away on June 2nd, at the end of the exposition, and no one knew when it would be seen again.

Still, not all those engaged in debate over the image aligned themselves either for or against authenticity. Some counselled patience: "One must wait for much more ink to flow on the sacred imprint found in the Turin relic." The ink did flow, but it is not likely that anyone at the time could have guessed in what quantities. The strip of linen cloth, and the riddle of its markings, was about to become the object of one of science's most prodigious—and meaningful—attempts at detection.

4

INTERLUDE:
THE YEARS BEFORE

If a direct, unbroken and documented link with Calvary existed for the Shroud of Turin there would never have been any doubt about its authenticity. Its provenance would have been its guarantee. There was no such link, however. The relic's history, it was true, stretched back into the mists of centuries, but there was a point at which the mist thickened into dense fog, obscuring its trail.

In 1898 the cloth had been at Turin for 320 years, closely guarded and venerated as the true Shroud. It had arrived in the city in 1578 as the property of the ruling House of Savoy, the family from which arose the kings of Italy. It had been brought there to accommodate the aging St Charles Borromeo, and the great saint had sunk to his knees in homage when he first viewed it through tear-dimmed eyes.

The years of the relic's stay at Turin were relatively quiet ones, with its public showings very rare. At first it was displayed annually, but such frequent handling and exposure, it was feared, would damage it unnecessarily. The 1898 Exposition was only the sixth time that nineteenth-century eyes had looked upon it. It had become the fixed custom to exhibit the Shroud only at great events of state and memorable happenings connected with the House of Savoy, especially marriages. Always, these expositions were accompanied by the most elaborate ceremonials, requiring many months to prepare.

Once, before it arrived at Turin, the relic had come perilously close to destruction. On the night of December 4th, 1532, fire broke out in the sacristy of the Sainte Chappelle at Chambery, France, where it was then kept. In minutes, the whole structure was a holocaust, with superheated flames licking around the silver casket containing the relic. Risking their lives two laymen, Fillipo Lambert and Guglielmo Pussod, and two Franciscan priests whose names have been lost, rushed into the inferno, smashed open the reliquary, and staggered from the burning building with the casket clutched in their arms. It was found that drops of molten silver had fallen on the cloth and burned through its forty-eight folds (the cloth was not rolled up until after its arrival at Turin; before that it was folded).

The silver had gone through only on the edges, missing the image almost entirely. For more than a year after the fire no attempt was made to repair the ugly holes that lined each side of the cloth. Then, in 1534, it was taken to the monastery of St. Clair, where the nuns, with extreme precision, sewed on patches.

A century before that fire, the cloth had led a rather

strange existence as the jealously maintained property of a French noblewoman, Margaret de Charny. This woman had kept possession of the relic in the face of civil and religious litigation, and had even incurred excommunication rather than give it up.

It had come into Margaret's family from the church of Lirey in Troyes, France. In 1418, when war was ravaging the land, the authorities at Lirey requested the Lord of the district, Margaret's husband, to protect their relic. It was turned over to him. A few years later he died and Margaret was in full charge of the cloth. She treated it with a passionate regard, even keeping it with her while travelling. Later, when peace had come again to Troyes, the priests at Lirey asked for its return. To their surprise, Margaret refused. It had belonged to her grandfather, she reminded them, and he had only loaned, not given, it to Lirey. She had decided to recall the loan, and that was that. Eventually, ecclesiastical courts decided in favour of Lirey and ordered the woman to give up the cloth. Again she refused—and kept on refusing until she was excommunicated. In 1452 she turned it over to the Duke of Savoy under circumstances that are not quite clear. It is known that Margaret received from him at least two French castles, with the mellifluous names of Mirabel and Flumet.

It was true that Margaret's grandfather had been the possessor of the cloth prior to Lirey. The records show that sometime between 1353 and 1356 Geoffrey I of Charny, then Lord of the district of Lirey, had presented it to that church. Exactly how and where he had obtained it no one seemed to know. Geoffrey was one of the most famous knights of his day in France, and it was generally supposed that he had acquired the Shroud as a spoil of war.

For the 1300 years that stretched backward from Geoffrey

to the crucifixion and burial of Jesus Christ the cloth could provide no indisputable testimony for its lineage. Throughout those dark centuries, ancient texts made only occasional references to a "shroud of Christ." Seven, possibly eight, eye-witnesses mentioned "burial linens of Christ," or a "winding sheet." But there was no sure way to link these old texts with the cloth of Lirey-Chambery-Turin.

At the beginning of this lost millennium, soon after the death of Christ, the four Evangelists had recorded the fact that a linen cloth had been used at the burial. Two of them, St. Luke and St. John, mentioned the burial clothes again in their accounts of the discovery of the empty tomb on Easter morning. St. John even seemed to attach some now-forgotten importance to them. Here are the words in which he described himself and St. Peter hastening to the tomb after being told that the body of Jesus was missing: "Peter, therefore, went out, and that other disciple, and they came to the sepulchre. And they both ran together, and that other disciple did outrun Peter, and came first to the sepulchre. And when he stooped down he saw the linen clothes lying; but yet he went not in. Then cometh Simon Peter, following him, and went into the sepulchre, and saw the linen clothes lying. And the napkin that had been about his head, not lying with the linen clothes, but apart, wrapped up into one place."

Here, Scripture drops the subject and, except for a cryptic mention in the apocryphal *Gospel of the Hebrews*, all reference to a shroud disappears from history for about 500 years. Regarding this time of silence, believers in the cloth's authenticity point out, with good logic, that the relic would have certainly been hidden away during the persecutions of the first three centuries. In 570, a pilgrim returned from Jerusalem reported that a shroud was kept in a monastery beside the

Jordan. St. Braulion, about sixty years later, spoke of a "winding sheet in which Our Lord was wrapped," and added that "The Scriptures do not tell us it was preserved, but one cannot call those superstitious who believe in the authenticity of this winding sheet."

In 670, Arculph, a French bishop on his way home from a pilgrimage to Jerusalem, was shipwrecked off the coast of Scotland. Eventually, he made his way to a monastery on the island of Iona and there dictated an account of all he had seen and heard on his trip. By such roundabout means the first definite *eyewitness* report of the existence of a shroud (whether or not authentic) was recorded. Arculph said that in Jerusalem he was present when a shroud was taken from a shrine and shown to a "multitude of people.' He had even been allowed to kiss it.

In succeeding centuries, other men spoke of a shroud: Venerable Bede, St. Willibald, St. John Damascene, the Emperor Baldwin. The *Song of the Voyage of Charlemagne to Jerusalem* mentions the shroud Jesus wore "when he was laid and stretched in the tomb." A letter of Alexius of Comnenos, some documents of Peter the Deacon, two catalogues made by pilgrims to Constantinople, a letter of William of Tyre— all refer specifically to a "shroud of Christ." Yet each of these antique texts—fewer than twenty in all—must forever remain isolated, like pinpoints of uncertain light in a long corridor of darkness. They cannot be connected with each other.

In 1204, Robert de Clari, chronicler of the Fourth Crusade, in describing what took place when Crusaders triumphantly stormed into Constantinople, wrote "There was a monastery known as Lady St. Mary of the Blachernes, in which was kept the shroud in which Our Lord was wrapped; on every Friday this was held out so well that it was possible to see the face of

Our Lord." But the darkness closed in again when he added: "Neither Greek nor Frenchman knew what happened to that shroud after the town was taken."

To fill in the gap between Constantinople and Geoffrey of Charny, there was a theory connecting the shroud de Clari had seen with the one that appeared at Lirey. At best, it was an amalgamation of questioned documents and guesswork. The relic, it was said, had remained at Constantinople after the fall of the city in the charge of a bishop who intended to transport it back to France personally. But the bishop died and the cloth disappeared. Supporters of the thesis pointed out that in the bishop's entourage were several men from Geoffrey's district, including at least one directly related ancestor. This left in the dark the Shroud's whereabouts from 1204 to 1353, and the hypothesis was not completely accepted even by the cloth's advocates. And there were Catholics as well as Protestants who rejected the Shroud altogether, finding it impossible to believe that it could have survived the wear of centuries even if it had been preserved at first. So wondrous a relic was simply too good to be true.

For Catholics, there was in this rejection no opposition to the will of their Church. While many Popes had declared a personal belief, nothing binding ever had been promulgated. Veneration of a relic, the Church had said long ago at the Second Council of Nicea, was by its nature purely relative; homage was paid to the person connected with the relic, not to the material object. In essence, the religious worth of such an act did not depend on authenticity. So long as there was no good reason for suspicion, the Church would permit, could even encourage, veneration of it. Where the Shroud of Turin, was concerned, Catholics, no less than Protestants, were free to think as they wished.

Part Two

5

THE PECULIAR AFFAIR
AT LIREY

Less than six months after the dramatic moment in Pia's darkroom, a middle-aged French priest stared at the pictures of the Shroud and slowly shook his head. A specialist in medieval lore, he had encountered this cloth before in his intellectual wanderings through the fourteenth century. He began a systematic rummaging through old documents and source books at the Bibliothèque Nationale and elsewhere. In 1899 and 1900 he published his findings and single-handedly almost destroyed the relic as an object of serious interest. The image on the Shroud, he contended, was a painting. It was a hoax, a forgery, concocted in the mid 1300's. He had the documents to prove it.

Cyr Ulysse Chevalier was something of a prodigy. Portraits of him depict dark, piercing eyes beneath a broad, square brow, and a certain tight-lipped seriousness. His pictures reinforced his reputation as a scrupulous scholar of scientific rigour. When, later in his life, one commentator labelled him as "the most learned man in France and perhaps in the entire world," the description seemed no more than apt. Born in 1841 at Rambouillet, he had entered the priesthood at the age of twenty-one and while still in the seminary was given the unusual honour of election to National Historical Society of France. Before he was thirty he had won an honourable mention at the French Congress of National Antiquities, and at thirty-six he became a knight of the Legion of Honour. Although his rise to prominence was based on a steadily mounting total of impressive writings, the one effort that catapulted him into the foremost ranks of world historians was his *Repetoire des Sources historiques du moyen age*. Begun in 1875 and finished in 1883, this was a monumental work that arranged and annotated almost the entire source material for the history of the Middle Ages. One section of it, the *Topobibliographie*, was characterized as being "the most extraordinarily documented work a single man could produce." Today, the *Repetoire* still holds an important place in the field.

Chevalier possessed, to an extreme degree, some of the rarer abilities of the historian. He seemed, for instance, to have an affinity for old documents, an instinct for finding original records that had lain undisturbed for centuries in the dusty darkness of archives, libraries and collections. His competence in deciphering the strange, cramped handwriting of dead ages was almost unique. In handling his sources, he possessed a truly impressive ability to digest mountains of material; for one of his studies, a history of the Dauphinate, he had carefully worked his way through more than 20,000 original documents.

By the turn of the century, Chevalier's influence in historical matters, especially in France, was prodigious. When he published his *Critical Study on the Origins of the Holy Shroud of Lirey–Chambery–Turin* in the autumn of 1900, his strongly worded opinion had the impact of a death-blow. Almost immediately, the article was reprinted as a pamphlet, with a sixty-page appendix giving readers the opportunity to scan the fifty documents on which he founded his decision.

From these documents we can piece together the outlines of the peculiar happenings at the church of Lirey that led Chevalier to his condemnation of the cloth. It is a bizarre little tale, plucked from the heart of another and greatly different era. There is about it a remoteness, a foreignness, that makes it difficult for the modern mind to grasp its whole meaning. But, as it relates to the Shroud, its implication is clear.

His Excellency, Peter d'Arcis, Bishop of Troyes, France, in 1389, was an ailing and deeply troubled man. Reports had begun to reach him of scandalous occurrences at one of the churches in his diocese—Our Lady of Lirey. It was said that a long strip of linen, bearing a double impression of a human body, was being shown to vast crowds of pilgrims at the church. While the exhibitors did not proclaim the cloth to be the true Shroud of Christ, the reports stated, such a rumour was circulating freely in private. Many people in the hordes that visited the church implicitly believed that the piece of linen, set on a high platform and flanked by torches, was Christ's real winding sheet. The atmosphere surrounding it seemed to confirm the notion; the ceremonial reverence surpassed even that accorded the Holy Eucharist itself.

Bishop d'Arcis felt sure that he *knew* this was not the real shroud. He remembered that about the year 1355, it had been declared spurious by one of his predecessors, who had branded it as nothing more than a clever painting. Scrupulously aware of his obligation to protect his flock from misrepresentation, d'Arcis ordered the Dean of the Lirey church to terminate the expositions, under pain of excommunication, until an investigation could be held.

The dean promptly replied that he had permission from a cardinal for the exposition, boldly filed an official appeal, and continued to show the cloth. Then, to thwart any attempt to seize the relic, the dean enlisted political help. He turned to the family of Geoffrey of Charny, the knight who had founded Lirey and donated the cloth. The elder Charny was dead, but his son, Geoffrey II, ruled the district. The son agreed to assume legal possession of the cloth and went even further: on one occasion he took part in the ceremonies, personally holding the cloth up for veneration. From the King of France, Geoffrey obtained permission to post a military guard of honour around the relic.

Humbly, d'Arcis entreated Geoffrey to suspend the expositions until a papal decision could be rendered. To this reasonable request, d'Arcis complained, the knight paid no attention at all.

Since the intrusion of Geoffrey had made the affair a civil matter, d'Arcis also turned to the King. This time he was heard. The King, aware of all the facts for the first time, ordered the cloth to be surrendered to the Bishop, and instructed the bailiff of Troyes to confiscate it. But the officer sent to the church returned empty-handed. The obstinate dean would not capitulate.

The stalemate between Bishop and Dean was broken unexpectedly in the summer of 1389. Geoffrey had secretly appealed to Pope Clement VII at Avignon for a ruling. (Clement VII was an anti-pope, the first in the Great Western Schism, but this fact does not have material importance in the story of the relic.)

Clement allowed the expositions to continue, with the proviso that the priests of Lirey must state, in a clear voice, that the cloth was a "copy or representation" of the Shroud of Christ. Clement also forbade the usual solemnities attending the exposition. There could be no lighted candles, no guard of honour. He imposed eternal silence regarding the subject on the surprised and agitated d'Arcis.

But d'Arcis would not be quiet. Towards the end of 1389 he composed for Clement's information a long report of the whole controversy. He held nothing back. The Dean of Lirey was acting with "fradulent intent and for the purpose of gain," he charged. Then he told what he knew of the cloth's origin:

"Some time since in this diocese of Troyes, the Dean of a certain collegiate church, to wit, that of Lirey, falsely and deceitfully, being consumed with the passion of avarice, and not from any motive of devotion but only of gain, procured for his church a certain cloth, cunningly painted, upon which, by a clever sleight-of-hand was depicted the twofold image of one man, that is to say, the back and front, he falsely declaring and pretending that this was the actual shroud in which our Saviour Jesus Christ was enfolded in the tomb, and upon which the whole likeness of the Saviour had remained thus impressed, together with the wounds which he bore."

The bishop of that earlier time, continued d'Arcis, had consulted with theologians, who had assured him that the cloth could not have been genuine since the gospels made no mention of any imprint, and that if it had been true it was unlikely that the Evangelists would have failed to record it.

"Eventually," wrote d'Arcis, "after diligent inquiry and investigation, he discovered the fraud and how the said cloth had been cunningly painted, the truth being attested by the artist who had painted it, to wit, that it was a work of human skill, and not miraculously wrought or bestowed." That earlier bishop had no better success against Lirey, d'Arcis stated, than he was having. Lirey had refused to surrender the relic and had hidden it away "for thirty-four years or there-abouts down to the present year."

D'Arcis ended his report with a strong statement; the words are those of an angry man: "I still oppose the said exposition until I have fuller instructions from your Holiness yourself, now better informed of the facts of the case. I would ask you . . . to take measures that such scandal and delusion and abominable superstition may be put an end to, both in fact and in seeming . . . to express horror of such superstition it be publicly condemned . . . I cannot fully or sufficiently express in writing the grievous nature of the scandal . . . "

Clement conducted no investigation. He merely ruled on the facts as they had been presented to him. On January 6th, 1390, he put his signature to three documents that ended the acrimony, although not in the way that d'Arcis had wanted. To Geoffrey he sent a letter reinforcing his previous decision to let the expositions continue, provided that it was always stated that the cloth was a "figure or representation." To Bishop d'Arcis he sent a letter reimposing perpetual silence, this time under pain of excommunication. To certain other ecclesiastics in the surrounding area he sent letters requiring them to oversee his decision in the matter.

With these three letters, the affair at Lirey comes to an

end. Bishop d'Arcis died in 1395 without leaving anything
further on record concerning his charge that the Shroud was a
painting and that the painter had confessed. No more documents came to light to reveal the details of the investigation
conducted by d'Arcis' predecessor. But, echoing across a
chasm of 500 years, those few short sentences composed by
the Bishop of Troyes, stood, like a challenging sentinel,
against the authenticity of the relic of Turin.

On the basis of the documents, Ulysse Chevalier declared
firmly that the image on the linen cloth was a painting executed in the Middle Ages. For him, the whole problem had
been settled by the testimony of Peter d'Arcis. It was no
accident, he concluded, that the mid-fourteenth century was
the precise point in history at which the relic's documentation
broke down. The negativity of the Pia photograph he dismissed as only apparent. In this, he was supported by Hippolyte
Chopin, a leading artist and photographer, who asserted that
the negative aspect was the result of a technical accident.
"The photograph proves nothing," Chopin assured him in a
letter, "absolutely nothing."

Public reaction to Chevalier's *Critical Study* was immediate.
Almost every serious reviewer referred to the thesis with
unstinted praise. Letters of congratulation poured in from
laity and clergy. In November, 1901, he received official
recognition: the Académie des Inscriptiones et Belles-
Lettres presented him with a gold medal amid the applause
of some of France's leading scholars. As 1901 closed, most of
those who had been interested in the Shroud turned from the
subject to more important matters. The cloth so carefully
preserved in the imposing chapel at Turin, they agreed, was
only another in that unfortunate line of false relics that had

plagued Christianity since the time of Constantine. The existence óf this one, at least, was at an end.

But even as Chevalier received his medal, a young biologist was at work in a laboratory at the Sorbonne. The results of his long and searching inquiry, a few months later, would throw the whole problem into the lap of science and Paris into a turmoil of argument.

6

PAUL VIGNON:
THE MAGIC KEY

The summit of 10,000-foot *L'Aiguille Meridionale d'Arves*, in the Dauphine Alps, is formed of a ridge about fifteen feet long and its sloping sides give it an uncanny resemblance to the roof of a cottage. On a summer day in the late 1880's, a young Frenchman balanced himself on this windy roof and gazed enraptured at the scene spread around him. His blue eyes sparkled with delight as they swept over the twinkling glaciers of the Rousses, the white tops of the Vanoise, the Pyramids of Viso, the stately Meije. To the north he could see the tremendous snow-mantled hulk of Mt. Blanc—the Monarch. He was the first man, he exulted, to look on the world from this vantage point; he was the first to scale the formidable *Meridionale*.

Paul Joseph Vignon, in his early twenties the day he stood on the top of *Meridionale*, was not alone in his fervent response to the challenge of the Alps. The last half of the nineteenth century was a time of mountain-madness. It had begun in 1854 with the first ascent of the Wetterhorn, and by 1865, the year of Vignon's birth, the fabled Matterhorn was conquered. The decade in between was the golden age of mountaineering and out of it a sport had been born. Each year thereafter, thousands of eager climbers, armed with rope and axe, stormed the big and little peaks that beckoned with a sudden fascination. Although Vignon was only one among these thousands, it is doubtful if many of them matched his single-minded drive against the calculated dangers of rock and snow and ice. Mountains became the ruling passion of his life. Year after year he returned to the Alps, not in search of fame as a conqueror, but merely to be climbing. It didn't matter greatly that a particular mountain might have been climbed once, or ten times. It was sufficient that *he* had not climbed it.

On some of these ascents, Vignon had for companion another dedicated mountaineer, a young Italian priest named Achille Ratti. Thus, the lure of the mountains had brought together, briefly, the two men who were to become the leading modern advocates of the Shroud of Turin. Years later they met again in a private audience room at the Vatican— Vignon as the moving spirit in the scientific study of the relic, and Ratti as the learned Pope Pius XI, who believed whole-heartedly in its authenticity.

Born at Lyon of a wealthy family, Vignon was attracted to science as well as the mountains, and especially to biology. With no necessity to earn a living, he had unlimited opportunity to indulge his twin interests. The climbing he pursued assiduously, even choosing to spend his military service with a famous troop of Alpine fighters. His marriage in 1892 didn't slow him down, although there must have been at least a twinge of disappointment when his eighteen-year-old bride declared her preference for level ground. His scientific studies during this time, in spite of the attraction he felt, were those of a dilettante, proceeding largely under impulse. But just before the turn of the century two events turned him towards a more orderly pursuit of knowledge and prepared him for his pioneer role in the story of the Turin enigma.

In 1895 he suffered a serious breakdown in health and nerves and was forced to convalesce in Switzerland for a year. This was a direct result of his unceasing attack on the mountains; he literally burned himself out in his headlong disregard for bodily care and his courting of the injuries or death that lay only a mis-step away. During this illness he took up painting as therapy and found in himself a talent for art. Thereafter, he showed the same dedication to brush and canvas, throwing himself into its study with all the devotion of a youthful, restless intellect. In a short time he was an accomplished painter, a member of a well-known art club, and was displaying his works in a Paris salon.

About a year after his recovery there occurred a fateful meeting between Vignon and one of France's foremost scientists, Yves Delage. Older by eleven years, Delage was a professor at the Sorbonne and a director of the Museum of Natural History. He stretched a guiding hand over Vignon's biological studies, igniting the spark of scientific intensity. And it was through Delage, an agnostic in religion, that the younger man, a Catholic, came finally to his work on the Shroud. In the end, it was Delage, ironically, who compelled the world of science to pay heed to the relic.

Paul Vignon first came under Delage's influence in 1897 when he accepted a staff position on *The Biological Year*, a magazine founded and edited by Delage. Soon, he was his assistant at both the Sorbonne and the Museum. The first fruits of the association were three original papers presented to the French Academy in 1899 and 1900; the questing spirit of the wealthy young man had found its goal. For the rest of his life Vignon remembered his debt to his friend, even in old age calling him "my master."

In 1900 Delage first showed Vignon the photographs of the Shroud taken by Pia. Despite Chevalier, his independent mind had seen in them something more than an ancient painting; something, at least, that demanded a better explanation than could be found in the yellowed letter of Bishop d'Arcis. He never wrote down anything about these first stirrings of a curiosity that were to rescue the Shroud from a premature oblivion. Today, his family says merely that he was "disturbed" by the photos.

Vignon had been aware of the pictures before, but, like so many others, had set them aside, after reading Chevalier, with little more than a glance. Now, encouraged by Delage, he saw the problem as a unique challenge. Here were pictures of a complex physical object that might or might not have been made by the hand of man. Surely, he reasoned, under close study the touch of a forger would betray itself somewhere in the multitudinous details. He resolved to make the study and to perform experiments where feasible. He would keep at it till he could put his finger on some fact by which he could brand the Shroud either completely false or undeniably genuine. Delage offered his help and placed his laboratory at Vignon's disposal.

In the early months of 1900, Vignon made a trip to Turin to enlist the help of Secondo Pia. Displaying the plates, Pia explained the methods he had used in taking the pictures, and supplied Vignon with copies on glass. Before he left, the young Frenchman made a discovery: two other men had made pictures of the relic during the Exposition. One was an "instantaneous" photo (snapshot in today's terms) by a priest; the other was a time exposure by a police lieutenant assigned to the cathedral. Neither of these was equal in quality to the Pia photos, but they did reveal the same negativity of the image, and so had a certain corroborative value. When he returned to Paris to begin his studies, Vignon had with him copies of these pictures as well as those of Pia. Dividing his time between the laboratory, his Paris apartment and the family chateâu at d'Herbeys, he spent the next eighteen months almost exclusively occupied with the problem of the Shroud.

In Vignon's view, the task facing him broke down logically into two stages. The first must concern itself solely with the nature of the imprints, the second with identification of the body. Whether he reached the second stage depended on the outcome of the first.

Initially, he would try to determine whether the imprint of the body on the cloth had been spontaneous or artificial. Were the stains in any way the product of a human hand, he asked, or were they the natural result of some law working without human intervention? He was aware of the several theories that advocates of the cloth had put forward. One was obviously nothing more than a guess that attributed the entire image to a simple blood transfer. Another was an attempt at a quasi-mystical explanation: the image had been made at the moment of the Resurrection by an electrical discharge from the suddenly glorified body of Christ. Vignon rejected both ideas. If the cloth really were authentic, he felt, the explanation should be more in keeping with existing, observable physical laws. If his first stage led him to the conclusion that the stains were artificial, then his work would be finished, the Shroud rejected. If, however, he was forced to admit that the stains were the result of a natural process, *and he could discover what that process was*, then he could go on to the second and final step, identification of the body.

For the first stage, he rigorously excluded from his calculations and hypotheses any reference to Jesus Christ. "We therefore eliminate," he later wrote, "all that may have been said or thought by man, in the course of the centuries, about the origins of this relic. For us it is simply a large piece of linen cloth . . . discoloured by time, worn and torn in places, half-burnt by fire and bearing upon its surface shadowy impressions." The blood-spots on the cloth, he judged, more properly belonged to the second stage; he would not treat them until he reached the question of identity.

In Delage's laboratory, Vignon set two pictures side by side. One showed the relic as it appeared naturally, to the eye. The other was the negative that depicted the noble-looking face and the contoured body. The scientist was struck, more forcibly than ever, by the fact that the Shroud was a mystery and would have remained one except for the miracle of the camera. Human eyes would never have probed its secret without the aid of photographic apparatus—"the magic key," he later called it. With this key, the secret of the relic—its negativity—lay open at last.

The stain-image was indisputably a negative. Was it possible, Vignon wondered, that an artist in the fourteenth century could have painted this negative? Was it possible that an artist in *any* century could paint *any* negative?

Vignon was an artist. He found it difficult to conceive how any man, regardless of ingenuity, could have painted so harmonious a picture *without seeing what he was doing*. And if the painting had been done in negative, that is exactly what would have been the case, since the artist would have had no means of checking his work. The impossibility of such a thing became fixed in Vignon's mind as the inherent absurdities tumbled over one another. The concept of a negative was unknown to the Middle Ages; it did not become part of human knowledge until the nineteenth century. But supposing someone in the Middle Ages had somehow known what a negative was—*why* would he have painted this way? So far as that old artist was concerned, no one would ever have been able to see the true value of his work!

As unlikely as the painting theory seemed, there were variations on it still to be considered. For instance, a clever fourteenth-century observer might have noticed that a body wrapped in a shroud would leave impressions of a sort, but not really a picture. Why couldn't he have determined which parts of the body would have touched the cloth and then have produced a painting based on this? He would have been making a negative without knowing he was doing so. The limbs and trunk, Vignon conceded for the moment, might have been done in this way. But the face? It was unthinkable that the perfection of that face could have been the result of chance. It was as absurd as believing that the *Mona Lisa* was an accidental arrangement of lights and shadows. And the hypothetical forger, again, would have been working blind.

A second variation was more complex; it required mulling over and a small experiment. One critic had suggested that the negativity of the marks could have been produced by a colour inversion in the chemical basis of an ordinary painting. Wrote the critic:

The flesh tints may have been painted with a mixture of white paint, which is an oxide of lead, or of zinc combined with reds, ochres or naturally tinted earths. The shadows may have been done with black paints mixed with ochres and natural or burnt earths, or even with bitumen . . .

The Holy Shroud passed through critical periods, such as the fire in the Sainte Chapelle in 1532, when the constitution of its colours must have been considerably modified. The oxides of lead in the light colours must have been clouded by the sulphur of mercury in the reds, or by external causes, such as one always sees at work in old paintings. The natural earths may have been calcined by the heat—the bitumen burnt, evaporated, vanished! All this is possible. What would now remain after the fire? A rude image whereon all the light tints which had been mixed with earth would be proportionally black and portions of which would be more or less obliterated.

Vignon knew that the Shroud was made of a very light and flexible material. He had verified that fact from persons who had actually handled the cloth. He had also seen evidence of it in the photographs. Accidental creases here and there in the material were represented as very fine lines—an unmistakable indication of the thinness of the cloth. The feasibility of the chemical inversion theory depended entirely on the presence of pigment. But how could such a light fabric have carried the necessary amount of pigment in the first place? And paint would have stiffened the cloth while it was still supple in all its parts. More important, for at least 500 years the relic had been rolled and unrolled, folded and unfolded, and carried from place to place. How could pigment possibly have adhered to it through all this handling, and adhered so well that not a trace of obliteration could be seen, especially in the face?

One small point, so evident it had been over-looked by others, decided Vignon against the chemical inversion idea. In such a case, the original figure on the cloth would have been an *obvious* oil painting—how, then, could it have fooled anyone in the fourteenth century? People in those distant times may have been naïve, but they weren't simpletons.

Here, at any rate, was something that could be tested. On a piece of linen, comparable in thickness to the Shroud, Vignon tried to paint a portrait. He found it necessary to use a very thin wash for pigmentation, with only a small quantity of lead. But with this mixture he could not obtain a picture. To get one, he had to paint over the first wash in light and dark tones. He finally achieved a passable but fragile result. Later, with the paint dry, he carefully folded his cloth. The paint scaled off at the folds and the picture was destroyed.

For Vignon the relic had become "a very remarkable—we may even say unique—object." No matter what Chevalier's documents said, the stain-image on the cloth had not come from the brush of a painter.

The scientist in Vignon, however, did not yet abandon all possibility of fraud. Might not forgers have gone about their work in some other way? Could the Shroud, for instance, have been fabricated by *contact* with a human body?

"Let us suppose we are going to take the print of the front view of a corpse lying on the ground. We should firmly press the cloth along the central line of the body and more lightly on the sloping surfaces, graduating our passes so that the general contours take form by degrees . . . the operator, we will say, has stretched the linen with great care, fixing the edges . . . he will be content to let the linen rest on the bridge of the nose, on the forehead and on the chin. Also on the cheek bones. To make the modelling possible, he will have made the cloth touch the sloping portions, such as the sides of the nose, lightly. He will have endeavoured to let it touch the lips with great delicacy . . . '' If such a thing could have been done in the fourteenth century, it was clear to Vignon, he should be able to repeat the process.

At the Sorbonne he enlisted the aid of two colleagues from the science department and explained his project. He would put on a false beard, then smear beard and face with a specially prepared pulverized red chalk. His colleagues, using a piece of albumen-coated linen, would take impressions; together, they would check the results with a camera. Vignon knew that some sort of negative would appear. What he was searching for specifically was any indication of the amazing perfection evident in the Shroud. Since the face presented the most difficulties, he would confine himself to that. It was not necessary to attempt the experiment on the whole body. What was true of the face would hold true for torso and limbs.

In Delage's laboratory, Vignon lay down on an operating table. The chalk was applied and the two men draped the first piece of cloth on his face. Gently, they pressed their fingers around the points of contact and allowed the linen to remain for some time. On lifting it they saw that it had retained the chalk, although the results were nothing more than a shapeless mass. When they photographed it, the negatives revealed a disappointingly grotesque rendering of the original. Twice more they tried, but each time, no matter how delicate their touch, the outcome was an unrecognizable caricature. The eyes were lowered almost to the level of the nostrils. Cheek-bones and mouth were out of place. The modelling was hard and sharp, totally unlike the rounded contours of an actual face. The three men agreed that the portrait on the Shroud could never have been produced in this way. Proportion, harmony and expression were the characteristics that gave the face on the relic its undeniable impact. These were the very qualities that were missing in the experimental cloths. Again Vignon's mind went back to the hypothetical forger in the fourteenth century: "If the forger had obtained a head no better than [ours] he would probably have been quite content with the result. His work would not have been criticized so long as no camera led to an investigation of it."

In truth, this experiment only confirmed a previous conclusion. He knew that contact alone could not render on a *flat* surface a true and undistorted impression of a *cylindrical* object. The flat surface would have to be wrapped around the cylinder and on being opened out again would unavoidably enlarge and distort the original object. The disparity would be even more apparent where the cylinder's surface was uneven, as in a human face.

Discarding the forgery-by-contact idea, the young scientist undertoook an anatomical comparison of the two images. As he expected, they coincided exactly in placement and general proportion. To the legs, he applied painstaking measurements. The length of a man's legs from kneecap to sole, he knew, should approximate twice the length of his head. On the Shroud, the head was not outlined with precision, so Vignon obtained the needed measurements in the usual way: twice the length from the inside corner of the eye to the chin. The final figures showed that the legs on the Shroud came within the accepted range for normal. They were only two centimetres longer than twice the length of the head. (Vignon avoided giving the probable height of the body itself, because of the vagueness of its limits. It has since been estimated at just over six feet.)

One thing had struck Vignon throughout his study. The hollows of the supine body were reproduced less strongly than the prominences. This was, of course, the factor that gave the marks their negative quality. But now, the deeper significance of this struck him. It meant that even in some places *where cloth and body had not touched*, the body still managed to leave an undistorted imprint. The cloth draped over the nose, for instance, would have touched the bridge of the nose and the outer portion of the cheek, but would not have touched the cheek nearer the nose. Yet this part of the face had marked the cloth, without having caused any of the distortion seen in Vignon's experiments.

Checking the rest of the figure, Vignon saw a pattern emerge: parts of the body that did not touch the linen, but lay within about one centimetre of it, left impressions. Parts that lay more than a few centimetres away did not leave any. Thus, it seemed, the stains were strong or faint or entirely absent, according to the distance of the cloth from the body. Scrutinizing every inch of the two figures, he saw that this pattern was unvaryingly consistent and, further, that in every instance it agreed perfectly with the dictates of anatomy.

The implication was inescapable: the stain-image had been made partly by contact and partly by *projection*. Some exudation from the body had succeeded in marking the cloth where it lay fairly close to the skin. Something emanating from the flesh had moulded the contours, so to speak, while the outline or design of the figure had been done by direct contact. What that *something* was, Vignon now proposed to discover.

In Vignon's time, especially in France, there was a generic term for the chemical concept he now began pursuing: *action at a distance*. A number of men had been interested particularly in the manner by which certain metallic gases and vapours could affect a sensitive plate. The subject was a short-lived off-shoot of the development of the camera; it had nothing to do with the Turin relic. But its brief existence provided Vignon with the knowledge he needed to probe further into the mysteries of the cloth.

What he wanted now was to produce an analogue of the Turin image. If he could achieve, on a flat photographic plate, a portrait with modelled contours through the action of vapours, then he would have demonstrated the validity of his contact-projection theory. After that, the way would be open for his final assault on the basic riddle of the Shroud. For help in the specialized field, he turned to René Colson, a professor at the *Ecole Polytechnique* in Paris, who had been experimenting with zinc vapours.

At Colson's suggestion, they began with the zinc. Each man selected a different object to work with, Vignon choosing a medal on which there was a head in low relief, and Colson a plaster cast of a head about four inches high. Their very first efforts met with success.

In the laboratory, Vignon carefully dusted his medal with a fine zinc powder, using a sable brush to remove the powder from the recessed portions. Some of the dust was left on the rim to form an outline. He placed the medal in a light-tight box, and then covered it with a photographic plate. He would wait twenty-four hours. Colson spread the zinc powder over the surface of his plaster head, then placed it in a light-tight box, on top of a photographic plate. The little statue touched the plate at forehead, nose and beard, showing a three-quarter profile. The men had used opposite methods in order to check the action of the vapours in both directions, upwards and downwards.

After twenty-four hours, Vignon extracted his plate and made a print from it. The results delighted him. Although the figure on the medal itself was in extremely low relief, traces of modelling could easily be seen in the plate, especially in the hairline and the lower jaw. It was Colson's plate, however, that provided a revelation. The face of a bearded man, seen a little from the side, was unmistakably present. The right side of the face was delicately highlighted, while the centre and left side faded away into the darkness. It resembled a Rembrandt painting in which the subject is seen in half-light or shadows. So well rendered was the impression, even to the brooding eyes, that Vignon felt the technique might have commercial possibilities: there was a certain "mysterious charm" about such pictures.

Convinced that they had found the method by which the stains were made, the two men hastened to uncover the materials involved. If the Shroud were considered as a photographic plate, then it must have had on its surface some substance that reacted to the bodily exudations. Here Vignon made an intuitive leap. The Shroud, he remembered, was said to have been brought from the East. It was known that Oriental peoples used aromatic substances in their burial rites. From references in ancient literature, Vignon concluded that the most common of these substances seemed to have been myrrh and aloes. He would begin with these.

Delving into the Old Testament in the original Greek, René Colson looked for directions on the funerary uses of these spices and found a Mosaic recipe for the preparation of sacred anointing perfumes. The Jews, he reported, pounded up the myrrh and aloes with pure olive oil to form a sort of unguent. In consistency, it became a semi-fluid paste. Vignon postulated that this unguent had been smeared on the cloth, thus in effect "sensitizing" the linen. This sensitive layer of myrrh and aloes had been discoloured by some chemical that had exuded from the body. What was that chemical?

Nowhere does Vignon record how much time passed between the asking of that question and the finding of the answer. According to Delage it was months. The length of time is not surprising; the investigators were breaking new ground. There were no guides. Week after week they discussed the problem, tearing apart the chemistry of the body then putting it back together again. It was Colson who came up with an inspired guess. He recalled that aloes contained two chemical principles, *aloin* and *aloetin*. The second of these oxidized readily in conjunction with alkalies. Perhaps, he theorized, it was an alkali in the body that had acted on the aloetin—ammonia, for instance. Feeling close to an answer, Vignon and Colson performed a quick experiment. Moistening a piece of linen with ammoniacal water, they dipped it into a mixture of oil and aloes. The cloth became a mottled brown and remained flexible. Depending on the amount of aloes in the oil, the mixture became either an encrustation in the texture of the cloth or a dye.

Ammonia and aloes . . . was that the secret of the Shroud?

For a test, Vignon took a plaster cast of a head, saturated it in ammoniacal water and laid on it a piece of aloes-impregnated linen. But he ran into unexpected trouble. The ammonia vapours were given off too fast, leaving only a general brown blur on the cloth. Some control was needed. The experiment was switched to a cast of a hand encased in a suede glove. With the pores of the glove filtering the vapours, an excellent imprint of the back of the hand resulted. Even the slight anatomical depression between the metacarpals was visible. On the thumb, the seam of the glove showed.

One problem now remained: how could a human body become the source of ammonia vapours?

Even before the question was framed, the minds of Colson and Vignon were reaching towards the answer. To their own conjectures, they added the opinions of qualified chemists. Rapidly now, everything fell into place. The human body contains urea. Under fermentation, urea is completely transformed into carbonate of ammonia, which regularly emits ammoniacal vapours. But how could a body be *coated* with urea? Through sweating. Normal sweat contains an elaborate mixture of chemicals, among them urea. And although normal sweat contains only a small amount of urea, in *morbid* sweat, the increase is astonishing. One noted authority assured Vignon: "Urea may be produced so abundantly in certain morbid sweats that it forms crystals on the surface of the body." A man in a crisis of pain, a man who had been tortured for any length of time before death would have been bathed in perspiration highly charged with urea.

Vignon's first stage was over. The stain-image on the Shroud of Turin had been produced naturally from the body of a man who, presumably, was dead.

7

PAUL VIGNON:

WHOSE BODY?

Blood. Dark little ripples and smears of clotted blood clinging to the fabric of the cloth. It was on the head, the chest, the hands and arms, the feet. To eyes familiar with the properties of free-flowing blood, the clots looked impressively real. But *were* they real?

Through a magnifying glass, Vignon peered intently at Pia's plates. The stains on the breast had the true aspect of a clot, formed by blood which had congealed below a newly opened wound. The curves and windings were exactly adapted to the variations of the chest's surface. More, the edges of the clot were clearly shown as a smooth, continuous line, not jagged as they would have been if a forger had poured liquid on to the cloth. A trickling liquid, Vignon established by experiment, would have run unevenly along the threads, drawn by capillary action. Under magnification, this could easily have been picked out. Yet the edges were smooth. The blood had somehow been *transferred* to the cloth after drying on the skin.

Especially interesting was the large drop, shaped like the numeral 3, over the left eyebrow. It appeared to spring from a definite point, indicated by a darker coloration. The flow had met the two normal wrinkles of the forehead and had spread itself out, at each of them, to form tiny horizontal pools. Then it continued, ending in a tear of blood close to the left eyebrow. There it dried. "Now any drop of blood," wrote Vignon, "drying thus upon a substance into which it does not penetrate, takes, when coagulated, a sort of basin-like shape . . . the border or brim of the basin is formed by the fibrin of the blood, containing the red corpuscles in its coagulum. The centre is composed of the serum, which in drying takes a dull brown tint. Here, as the liquid part of the serum evaporates, the convexity of the centre is depressed. The contour of the drop of blood preserves, however, the same shape as it had when it was fresh." This exact condition could be seen in the drop on the forehead, he said. It was bordered by a dark edge, but its centre was of a lighter tint. The fragile bloodstain showed entire faithfulness to scientific detail.

Having previously kept the name of Jesus Christ completely out of sight, Vignon was now ready to test the claim that connected the relic with the crucified Messiah. How, he asked, did the multitude of details, plainly evident, on the cloth, accord with the circumstances of the Passion, death and burial of Christ? Four men—one of them an eyewitness—had preserved in the Gospels certain facts about the event. How well would the testimony of the Shroud fit these facts? With the help of Colson, he studied the interplay of evidence, point by point.

Christ had been crowned with thorns. On the relic,
distinct brown stains could be seen all around the head, even
among the hair, as though blood had gushed suddenly from a
puncture. This crown had been unique: in all history there
was no record of any condemned man other than Christ having
been maltreated this way.

Christ's side, while he hung on the cross, had been pierced
by a spear or lance. On the relic, the right side of the breast
displayed a lentil-shaped wound. From the quantity of blood
that had caked below it, Vignon thought the blow must have
severed some of the main vessels, even entered the heart.
Such a blow would have been fatal, if the man receiving it
had not been dead already.

Nails had been driven through Christ's hands. On the relic,
blood had flowed from a wound at the back of what appeared
to be the wrist. The position of the wound in the wrist, and
not in the middle of the palm as tradition demanded, was
arresting. The anomaly had been noted before, of course, and
one cleric had offered the explanation that the nail had, in fact,
entered the palm, but obliquely, and had emerged at the
wrist. However, that hypothesis did not appeal to Vignon
and he eventually decided that the wrist-wound provided one
of the more important and striking proofs of the cloth's
authenticity. "Every time we find in the Holy Shroud some
strangeness," he noted, "some departure from tradition, we
may feel assured that such strangeness, such departure, can
never have been knowingly done by a forger . . . Sometimes,
as we shall see, such an apparent error is found in reality to be
an absolute truth."

Anatomy proved, he insisted, that the nails *must* have been
driven into the wrists, *not* the palms. A nail in the palms could
not have sustained the weight of the body. The wounds would

have enlarged quickly and would have torn through the ligaments at the base of the fingers. But a nail in the wrists would have fixed the body securely to the cross. The weight, then, would have been on the extremities of the metacarpal bones. Although the Gospels used the word "hands" in referring to these wounds, there was no difficulty about their location in the wrists; in all ages the wrist had been accepted as part of the hand.

On the relic, the blood from these wrist wounds had flowed along the forearms. But this flow was not connected directly to the wound—there was a blank space of about two inches before the trickles began. No artist had ever depicted flowing blood unconnected to its source. Why this separation? Here, Vignon decided, was another one of those "errors" that fairly shouted for authenticity. From the way the hands were folded on each other, it was easy to see that the cloth draped over them would not, in reality, have come in contact with the arm at this point.

Christ had been nailed by the feet as well as the hands, and on the cloth there was a mass of bloodstains attesting to the fact. In this blood Vignon detected two kinds of stains. One was a transfer of dried blood, but the other had resulted from a *flow* of blood or a reddish serum. The fact that it had flowed on to the cloth was obvious from the jagged appearance of the edges. To Vignon's mind, this conjunction of two different stains could be explained only by the extraction of the nails after the body was taken from the cross. Blood would have dried on the feet during the crucifixion, and fresh blood or serum would have flowed for a while after removal of the nails.

What gripped him most, it seemed, were the marks of scourging. Scripture reported that Christ had been bound to a pillar and lashed unmercifully. On the relic could be seen tiny, contusion-like spots, in the shape of dumb-bells, all over the body. They stood out especially on the back and buttocks, the thighs and calves. "At the worst part," observed Vignon, "the skin has been cut and the blood has oozed forth, otherwise the spot is pale in colour; it is certainly a mark produced by serum with which the linen has been wetted."

Under magnification he could see that all these marks were not the same, but were subtly differentiated. Some were only half dumb-bells, some seemed to have cut more deeply than others—the shapes in general showed minute variations. They could only have been inflicted, he felt certain, through a violent striking of the flesh, probably by metal bits of some kind, attached to cords. The *Dictionary of Roman and Greek Antiquities* supplied him with the historical counterpart of just such a murderous weapon: the Roman *flagrum*. "It was composed of many chains," ran the account, "to each of which a metal button was attached, having a short handle like a postilion's whip."

But it was not only the appearance of these marks that intrigued the scientist. He found their "general distribution and direction in relation to the body" remarkable. On the back view, in particular, they spread out from a horizontal axis, about waist-high, fanning upward on the back and downward on the thighs and calves. The peculiar arrangement was strongly marked on both left and right sides, telling plainly of two whip-wielders behind the sufferer who delivered their blows alternately. If there had been any lingering doubt in Vignon's mind about the tendency of the evidence he was weighing, these scourge-marks erased it. It was simply inconceivable, he said, that an artist attempting to reproduce the marks of scourging on a human body could have imagined a system of scars so complicated.

The marks led him to another consideration—the body in the Shroud unmistakably had been naked. Some fifteen of the welts left by the whip could be counted on the parts, near the pelvis, that any loin-cloth would have veiled. No forger or artist of the Middle Ages, Vignon emphasized, would have dared show a nude Christ in a work destined for public display. This nudity of the image, even by itself, he thought, went far towards proving authenticity.

Although by now Vignon had tacitly accepted the Turin relic as genuine, he knew that if any positive evidence in the Gospels denied it, then it could not be what it seemed to be. But a lengthy study of all the pertinent passages only confirmed his belief. It was with satisfaction that he wrote: "A closer agreement between the results of a physicochemical study, made after a lapse of twenty centuries, and the testimony of those who were actual eyewitnesses of the event, could not be desired."

St. Matthew, the oldest of the four narrators, witnessed the use of a shroud: "When Joseph had taken the body, he wrapped it in a clean linen cloth and laid it in his own new tomb . . . " Saints Mark and Luke corroborated Matthew, all three using the word *sindon* to describe the linen cloth. St. John caused some difficulty by using two different words to describe the grave cloths (*othonia* and *sudarium*), but it was also St. John who, alone, referred to the spices required by Vignon's theory: "And there came also Nicodemus . . . and brought a mixture of myrrh and aloes, about an hundred pound weight." (This was almost seventy pounds, in modern terms, according to one authority.)

To support authenticity, Vignon had to be sure that the burial had been *provisional*. If the complete, or *definitive*, rites had been performed the body would have been washed, destroying all possibility of its having left impressions. Further, the corpse then might have been swathed in linen strips and not enveloped in a large shroud. Vignon reasoned that there had been a hasty burial with the intention of later completion. Although none of the Evangelists go into much detail about Christ's interment, Vignon found evidence for his view in a close reading of them. St. Matthew says: "It was already late, as it was the preparation day, that is the eve of the Sabbath . . ." It would have required time, insisted Vignon, for Joseph of Arimathea to complete the necessary formalities with Pilate, to procure the needed utensils and grave clothes, to perform the difficult task of removing the body from the cross, and to carry it to the tomb where the burial rites could be undertaken.

"Certainly," he argued, "by the time that Christ had been taken down from the cross, the day must have been nearly done; moreover, it was Friday, the eve of the Sabbath during which day all work was forbidden. The Sabbath began at six or half-past six, in the month of April. Therefore it is certain that Joseph of Arimathea and Nicodemus would not have had time to perform a regular burial. They would have been obliged to do what they could in the limited time at their disposal, and postpone till the day after the Sabbath (our Easter day) the completion of the unfinished obsequies."

There was confirmation, he asserted, in the fact, as recounted by the Evangelists, that the Holy Women went to the tomb on Sunday morning carrying spices and ointments. What had brought these women out so early if not to complete the burial?

Of course, the women had found the tomb empty. St. Peter, informed by them in high excitement, had hastened there with St. John. Inside the sepulchre Peter saw "the linen clothes lying.'' What became of the Shroud from that moment on? Vignon ventured no guess. He contented himself with: "We must not forget that amongst the Jews all linen used in burial was held to be impure, and the fact of its preservation would therefore be a most carefully guarded secret amongst the disciples.'' He had started as an impartial observer. He had now become an ardent advocate of the relic. He believed he had largely penetrated its mysteries. But in his thoroughness he turned, at the last, to one final hypothesis that would still deny the cloth's connection with Christ.

Suppose, someone had suggested, that another man some-time in the course of the early centuries—some poor criminal —had been crowned with thorns, scourged, crucified and lanced in the side. Why couldn't the Shroud of Turin be *his* winding sheet? A marvellous coincidence? Yes. But who was to say it couldn't happen? Vignon didn't even bother to calculate the enormous odds against it. His answer was more direct and convincing—and its implications devastating. There was one essential condition, he said, for the production and retention of the imprint on the cloth: "The body would have remained in contact with the cloth for too short a time to allow of putrefaction. If corruption set in, any impression pre-viously made would be, *ipso facto*, destroyed.'' There was no sign of corruption on the linen.

8

YVES DELAGE:
AN UNACCUSTOMED
SILENCE

A buzz of astonishment went through the intellectual circles of Paris in the early months of 1902. Word had filtered out that Yves Delage, the agnostic, would present to the Academy of Sciences a report entitled: "The Image of Christ Visible on the Holy Shroud of Turin." It was not only that a rationalist free-thinker was involved, although that was cause enough for perplexity, but the austere halls of the Academy had never before echoed to the name of Jesus Christ. It was then composed to a great extent of religious sceptics, and in any case its work lay in quite other directions.

Basic to the surprised reaction was Delage's position of

eminence. When Paul Vignon first met him, Delage was near the zenith of a career that had begun sixteen years before. His fields were zoology and biology, but he was equally at home in physics and mathematics. The subjects of heredity and evolution claimed a large share of his attention and for a while he engaged in an amiable dispute with Charles Darwin. Contemporaries remarked wonderingly on his precision and tenacity in pursuit of facts, the fertility of his imagination, the daring and flexibility of his approach. Yet his mind was not chained to the microscope and the dissecting table. Among his voluminous writings there is a slim collection of delicate and perceptive poetry and, perhaps more revealingly, an incisive dissertation on the nature of comedy.

He was a man of quiet habits, but he had a gusto that occasionally bubbled to the surface. It prompted, for instance, his quixotic participation in a bicycle race at the age of forty-six. He was no racer, but he had been a cyclist all his life, and it was his family's habit to pack a lunch and go wheeling off to the serenity of some little-travelled country road. In 1901, when the annual race from Paris to Cannes, a distance of 160 miles, was announced, he decided to enter. Wifely logic could not dissuade him: "What others can do, I can do," he said with a flourish, forgetting the handicap of his years. He arrived at Cannes far in the rear of the competitors, but he finished the race. Scarcely able to stand, he managed a proud "I did it!" Two days in bed followed. It was later that same year that he was raised to a seat in the pontifical Academy of Sciences.

In 1906 tragedy struck him; he began to lose the sight of his left eye. By 1910 he was totally blind. Without sight, he was cut off from laboratory work, so he turned abruptly from his labours in natural science to the then new field of psychology.

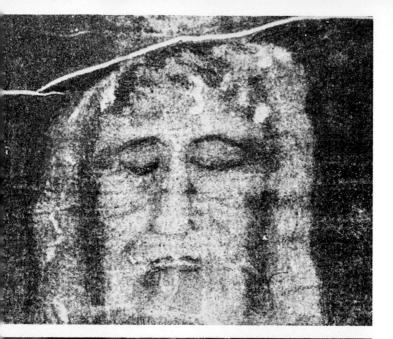
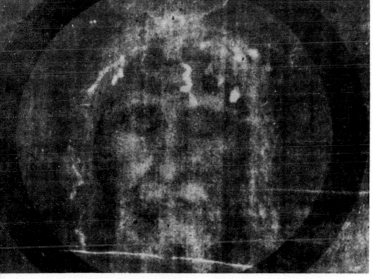

2. Two views of the face on the Shroud as it appears in photographic negative. The white trickle on the forehead is a bloodstain in negative.

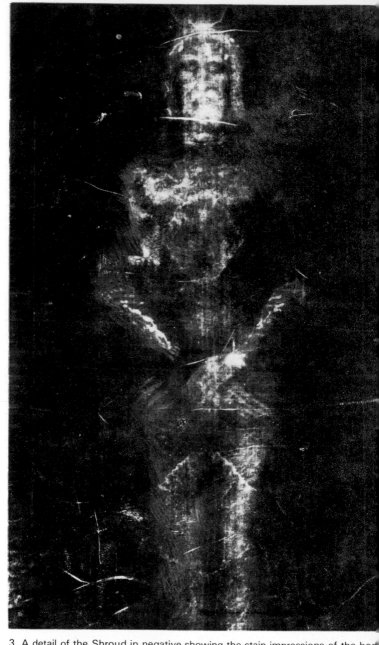

3. A detail of the Shroud in negative showing the stain impressions of the bod

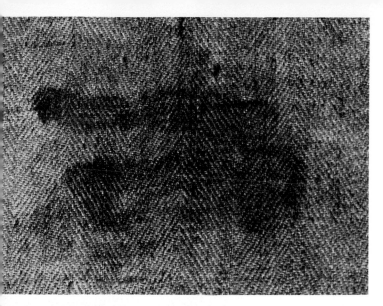

A detail of the Shroud showing the blood from the wrist wound, and the
ture of the cloth.

hotographer Leo Vala with a picture in profile of the three-dimensional model
roduced from photographs of the face on the Shroud.

6. The Shroud as it appears to the eye of the observer.

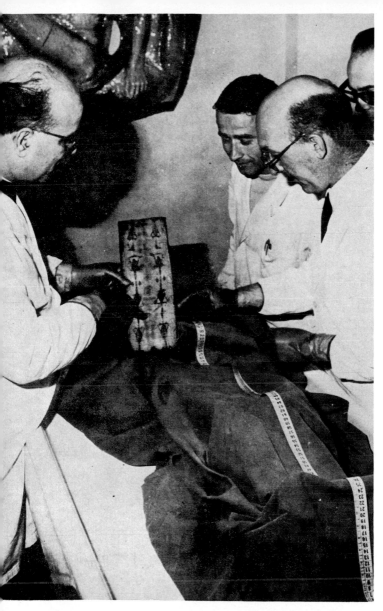

Monseigneur Giulio (left), an archivist at the Congregation for Bishops and Professor Nicolo Miani, a sculptor and scholar of anatomy, during a practical attempt to determine the height of the figure on the Shroud. They concluded that the figure's height was 5ft 4ins.

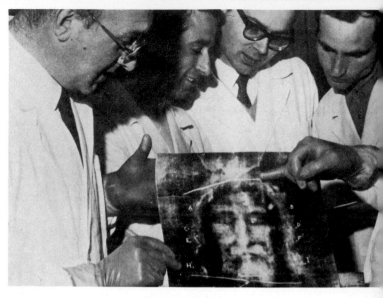

8. Msgr. Guilio Ricci and Prof. Nicolo Miani with the photograph on which they worked some of their calculations.

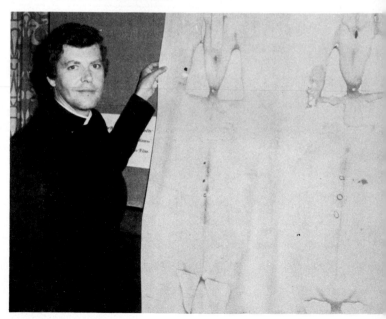

9. Father David Sox with an exact replica of the Shroud, compiled by computer

10 & 11. The Shroud on view to the public in the Duomo of Turin.

12. The Orthodox Bishop of Leningrad, M. Nikodim, visits the Shroud.

Only two months before his death he finished the last page of
a massive pioneer work on the psychology of the dream. He
had written the manuscript himself, using a specially constructed writing board to guide his pencil. From this, his
daughter-in-law had made a fair copy for the printer.

Born a Catholic and married in the church, Delage had
early in life turned to agnosticism. He had consented to a
religious wedding for his wife's sake, but his children were
not baptized and all his life he remained sincere in his belief
that humanity was restricted to its material existence, unable
to know anything about God, or even if there was a God.
From this, of course, he necessarily rejected the divinity of
Jesus Christ.

Among all the thousands of words written about his achieve-
ments, at his death and afterwards, the part he played in the
Shroud controversy at the start of the century is given small
mention. It was a brief part, based wholly on scientific
grounds. It had no connection with the main body of work
for which he was known and honoured. Yet nothing else
in his sixty-six years so well marked his true worth. For,
while he did not believe in a divine Christ, he still admitted
the historical existence of Jesus, and believed that the marks
on the relic had been made by His dead body. In the face of
the bitter attacks that followed his bold espousal of the
relic's cause, he held to that belief unwaveringly. Such in-
tegrity and clarity of mind concerning the two most
agitated questions of the day—religion and science—were
not exactly common in *fin de siècle* Paris. They are not common today.

Delage had conferred with Vignon at every step, and
agreed completely with his conclusions. Just how the results
were to be made public was a topic exhaustively discussed

between the two men. Vignon, indeed, had already revealed some of his ideas to the people he thought would be most concerned—Ulysse Chevalier and his supporters. In October of 1901, Vignon had attended a special meeting at the home of Chevalier, in Romans, presided over by the Bishop of Cahors. This was before Vignon had succeeded in tracking down the chemical explanation of the imprints, and he seems to have later regretted the impulse. In a letter he says: "I was far from getting across to M. Chevalier's guests in two hours the stages of an argument which for some long months has been submitted to the verifications of a host of competent judges . . . let us continue a difficult inquiry in silence; let us avoid divulging the details prematurely . . ."

Vignon was putting his results into book form and this seems to have moved Delage to suggest a full-scale report to the Academy. As a member, he had the privilege of bringing before that group whatever he judged of sufficient interest. Vignon, knowing that publicity for the shroud would inevitably follow, accepted the daring suggestion with alacrity. He began preparation of the notes to be used by his friend.

At three o'clock on the afternoon of April 21st, 1902, the regular weekly meeting of the Academy of Sciences was called to attention by its president. A crowd of well over 200 people had managed to find space in the long, rather narrow, high-ceilinged room. At green-covered tables down the middle of the floor, eighty or so venerable *Academiciens* occupied assigned places. On long benches ranging around the walls, the public squirmed for space. Among these, in addition to writers and reporters, were scholars, both laymen and clergy, of nearly every description; somewhere on these benches sat

Paul Vignon. Dominating the scene was the large desk, or
bureau, of the president and his secretaries.

The French Academy was, without doubt, the foremost
scientific body in the world at the time, and this room was
steeped in long tradition. Statues and paintings of the greats of
French science and literature peered down from the wooden
panelling, emphasizing a sense of continuity with the past that
was almost tangible. Only a decade before, one of these
weekly meetings had witnessed the first presentation of the
basic electrical phenomena that had led to wireless tele-
graphy. Interestingly it was before a similar gathering in 1839,
that the technique of photography itself was first given to the
world by Daguerre. There still lingered in the atmosphere
dramatic memories of Louis Pasteur, especially of the famous
meeting at which he had announced his vaccine for rabies.
That had been nearly fifteen years before—the last time the
hall had accommodated such a crush of listeners.

As the voice of the secretary rattled out the minutes of the
previous week, a hum of conversation welled from the members at the tables. Some rose from their chairs to buttonhole
colleagues. When the first scientific reports got under way, the
noisy inattention continued, but the president made no move
to obtain quiet. This *brouhaha* (in the colourful word of the
Academy's official history) was a long established custom and
was, if anything, typically French. With so many of the leading
minds of the country in the same room, an unexpected spark
might be struck from even the smallest interchange of ideas.
Conversation was thus allowed among members at all times.
In any case, the work of the meeting was published in
the official *Comptes Rendus* where it could be consulted at
leisure.

When the name of Yves Delage was called, at about four

o'clock and after several members had spoken, an utter and unaccustomed silence descended on the gathering. Amid the hush, the bearded and black-suited Delage moved towards the president's desk. Under his arm he carried enlargements of the face on the Shroud. Attendants hurriedly supplied a blackboard and table.

In crisp tones that carried to the extremities of the hall, Delage told his listeners of the existence of a strip of linen supposed to be the Shroud of Christ. He briefly detailed its history, and outlined the facts of the exposition of 1898 and the pictures taken by Secondo Pia. Showing the photographs, he explained the problem of negativity that had given rise to the whole question and had led him and his colleagues into the fields of chemistry, physics and physiology in their pursuit of the truth.

"The question poses itself," he said, "as to how this image was made."

He sketched Vignon's painstaking studies and their conclusion that the stain-image could not possibly be a painting, either directly or by inversion of colours. He launched into a description of the naturalism of the bloodstains, the marvellous complexity of the wounds left by the flogging, the surprising nudity of the image, the unusual position of the wound in the wrist, and the delicate modelling of the whole figure. The picture of the face, he said, was extremely realistic —impeccable, without a weakness. It even showed "characteristics which are not found in any iconographic reproductions" of the fourteenth century, or in fact in those of any other period.

"For these and other reasons," he continued, "the conviction results that the image of the shroud is not a painting made by the human hand, but that it has been obtained by a physicochemical phenomenon. And the scientific question which presents itself is this: how can a corpse yield an image on the shroud which covers it, causing it to reproduce its shape with the details of the facial features?"

He answered his own question with a circumstantial description of the work done in his laboratory by Vignon and Colson. "The image," he said with precision, "is an approximately orthogonal projection, a little diffuse, and the intensity of the shade in each point varies in inverse sense with the distance to the corresponding point on the corpse. This intensity decreases very rapidly in proportion to the increase in distance, and becomes nil when the latter reaches a few centimetres." The chemical agents involved, he added, were the aloetin layer in aloes and the carbonate of ammonia fermenting in the urea-charged sweat.

Pausing, he looked round. "Must I speak of the identification of the person whose image appears on the shroud?" he asked. No answer was expected. Acutely aware of what he was about to say, the question was a way of sliding into difficult terrain, of softening the impact of the name of Jesus.

The truth could be reached, he continued, along two separate lines of inquiry. On the one hand, there was the Shroud telling plainly of a victim who had been crucified, flogged, pierced in the side and crowned with thorns. On the other hand, there was the story of Christ's Passion, telling just as plainly of a man who had suffered those very punishments. "Is it not natural to bring these two parallel series together and tie them to the same object?"

Glancing at his notes, he went on. "Let us add to this, that, in order for the image to have formed itself without being ultimately destroyed, it was necessary that the corpse remain in the shroud at least twenty-four hours, the amount of time needed for the formation of the image, and at the most several days, after which a putrefaction sets in which destroys the image and finally the shroud." He paused again. He had gone as far as he could without a wrench to his own conscience. His next words were carefully phrased. "Tradition—more or less apocryphal, I would say—tells us that this is precisely what happened to Christ; dead on Friday and—disappeared—on Sunday."

Then, gravely, Delage made his affirmation: "The man of the shroud was the Christ."

In concluding his report he declared that, though the Shroud itself had not been tested in the inquiry, the photographs formed a sufficient and legitimate basis for study, and it was, in fact, a technique accepted by many branches of scientific investigation. Examination of the Shroud itself was the next logical step, he said, and he proposed that the Academy should appoint a special committee to intercede with the Italian authorities for the necessary permission.

His talk had lasted about a half-hour and had been received in absolute quiet. As he returned to his place, the spectators on the public benches found their voices again and a murmur of excited discussion broke out. Gesticulating groups formed noisily around Vignon and Delage.

The president adjourned the meeting with the announcement that a secret committee would go into session immediately. Fifteen minutes later the Academy returned its answer to the proposal for intervention: declined on the ground that the relic belonged to the Royal House of Italy; only if the Italian King made the request would it be entertained. Moreover, as it then stood, the entire problem was beyond the scope of the Academy's aims.

But the two scientists were satisfied. Soon the whole world would be aware of the Shroud of Turin.

Seldom has Paris witnessed such a convulsive reaction as that which followed Delage's lecture. Newspapers blared forth the story in column after tightly-printed column. Before the year was ended, Parisian presses poured out at least twenty-five magazine articles and ten books dealing with the relic. Of this mass of material, about half was in favour and half against, but almost nobody was without an opinion.

It was the same around the globe, though less vociferously. In America, the *New York Times* front-paged its account in rather primitive journalese:

HOLY SHROUD TESTED

French Scientists claim that it
possesses photographic properties
—their conclusions accepted

(Special to the New York Times)
Copyright 1902

LONDON, April 26th—The strangest story of the week is that relating to M. Paul Vignon's photographic experiments with the Holy Shroud, preserved in the cathedral at Turin, and the most astounding feature of that is the seeming acceptance of the results as scientific, both by the esteemed *Lancet* and the London *Times*. The latter declares that the position of M. Vignon and his associate professor, M. Yves Delage, in the scientific world, to be such as to insure for their conclusions the most careful appreciative consideration from men of science everywhere. Both Journals seem to accept this shroud as a veritable relic, and assume that the use of oils and aloes upon it nineteen centuries ago caused it to act as a photographic plate on which a faithful picture was recorded . . .

The sober *Scientific American*, which in 1898 had been more interested in Pia's use of electric light than in the Shroud, gave the story a whole page, reprinting verbatim an article from the British *Nature*, adding only a new lead taken from the body of the piece.

The Lancet, that most esteemed of British medical journals, reported the event with unexpected tolerance, although it mistakenly attributed both the taking of the pictures and the delivering of the report to Vignon. "An exact image," it agreed, "even to minute details such as wounds produced by the thorns and the marks of the blood-drops, and of flagellation by whips of a definite kind, is not by any means beyond the bounds of probability. It is an intensely remarkable and interesting instance of the light which the very latest developments of scientific research may throw on traditions and controversial matters of history."

In Paris, though, the storm clouds billowed. The French capital, characteristically, could not make up its mind whether it was faced with a legitimate problem or a hoax. *Le Figaro*, one of its popular dailies, plumped for authenticity. In the lobby of its building, it set up a huge display around a blow-up of the face on the Shroud and announced proudly that thousands of visitors were viewing it daily. Later, it had smaller copies on sale for three francs apiece. As the story developed, it printed a running commentary, rounding up opinions favourable to the relic. Finally, it scored an exclusive interview with the Cardinal of Turin. Its rival, *Le Temps*, struggling to keep up, matched every move.

The Paris edition of the *New York Herald*, in its lead story on April 23, carried these excited headlines:

PHOTOGRAPHS OF CHRIST'S
BODY FOUND BY SCIENCE

Reddish-coloured stains on the
Holy Shroud preserved at
Turin are negatives

EXTRAORDINARY REVELATIONS

Curious chemical process by
which the actual aspect
of the Saviour has
been recorded

"The image," ran the story, "is startling in its awful realism." Then, four days later, the *Herald*, with true objectivity, gave equal space to the opponents:

SCIENTISTS DENOUNCE
TURIN'S HOLY SHROUD

M. Leopold Delisle tells
Academy of Inscriptions
the claim has not
been proved

The account reported a meeting of the Académie des Inscriptiones et Belles-Lettres, held on April 26th, at which Delisle, director of the Bibliotheque Nationale, "voiced the denunciation of what he claims to be an imposture," and reminded the public of the work of Ulysse Chevalier.

No real pattern was traceable in the newspaper reaction; it ranged from outright acceptance to scathing charges of chicanery. *La Fronde*, especially, picked up the old rumour about Pia and repeated it. In a feature story that covered most of the front page, it risked a charge of libel by baldly concluding that the only possible answer to the problem was that the Turinese photographer had fraudulently retouched the original negative. The journalistic hubbub continued until the middle of May, when the public's attention was suddenly diverted by the tragic volcanic explosion at Martinique in which the entire town of St. Pierre was wiped out. The heated discussion wasn't ended, however, it only moved over into the scholarly magazines.

Neither Delage nor Vignon escaped personal abuse in the imbroglio. Delage was derided as a betrayer of science and a traitor to his religious convictions. His only answer to the insults appeared in the *Revue Scientifique* in a letter to Charles Richet, the editor.

When I paid you a visit in your laboratory several months ago to introduce you to M. Vignon . . . had you the presentiment of impassioned quarrels which this question would arouse in the press . . . ?

I willingly recognize that none of these given arguments offer the features of an irrefutable demonstration; but it must be recognized that their whole constitutes a bundle of imposing probabilities, some of which are very near being proven . . . a religious question has been needlessly injected into a problem which in itself is purely scientific, with the result that feelings have run high, and reason has been led astray. If, instead of Christ, there were a question of some person like a Sargon, an Achilles or one of the

Pharaohs, no one would have thought of making any objection . . . I have been faithful to the true spirit of science in treating this question, intent only on the truth, not concerned in the least whether it would affect the interests of any religious party . . . I recognize Christ as a historical personage and I see no reason why anyone should be scandalized that there still exist material traces of his earthly life.

In June, Delage reaffirmed his faith in the Shroud by presenting to the Academy some work of a Belgian scientist confirming the experiments of Vignon and Colson. With this, his public connection with the Shroud ceased and he turned to his duties at the Sorbonne and the government biological laboratory at Roscoff, of which he had been named director. Through Vignon he maintained a private interest in the fortunes of the relic.

Vignon's book, *The Shroud of Christ*, made its appearance in May. It was an expanded and well-illustrated narration of all the points covered at the Academy. The artist in Vignon could not resist an added touch: a separate chapter lengthily compared the face on the relic with the conceptions of Christ envisioned by history's greatest artists. None of them, he felt, could compare with the simple grandeur of the dim portrait on the cloth. The book sold out immediately and was revised and reprinted within a month. A translation came out in England and America soon after.

If the attackers had called Delage a traitor, they dismissed Vignon as a self-deluding fanatic and his book as worthless. A review in *Nature*, a highly respected periodical, is only a mild example of the reception the book received from the more rabid sections of the opposition. "Whether the relic described, figured and discussed in this handsomely-got-up volume is the veritable shroud that enwrapped the body of Christ is a question which need not be seriously considered in the columns of a scientific publication . . . Dr. Vignon is either the victim of credulity or he had overdone his evidence to such an extent as to have damaged his own reputation as an expert scientific witness . . . to the reviewer it reads like an antiquarian dissertation ending in a pseudo-scientific anticlimax.''

To all such, as well as to the more balanced efforts at refutation, Vignon calmly responded with a number of magazine articles that reiterated his position and the steps leading to it.

Perhaps it was the spirit of the times, perhaps the undoubted complexity of the problem or the continued inaccessibility of the relic—whatever the reason, the tide turned once more against the Shroud. Where there should have been —in view of all that had happened—a state of suspended judgment, there was instead, especially among the historians led by Chevalier, renewed condemnation. Some attempt was made to meet Vignon on a scientific level, but it was desultory. In any case, it was the ghost of Bishop Peter d'Arcis that finally decided the issue. His centuries-old charge of fraud, in the minds of historians, admitted of no dispute. Before long, all the standard reference works branded the Shroud of Turin as spurious, most of them even omitting any reference to the literature in its favour.

A biblical disagreement also sprang up, with certain exegetes holding that the words of St. John could not be interpreted to mean a large linen sheet or a provisional burial. Other critics cited some forty more supposed shrouds of Christ in existence at various places. This fact was meaningless, the advocates countered, since it was known that these were either obvious copies of the Turin relic, or merely pieces of unadorned cloth. Simple assertion of the fact, though, muddied the controversy still further.

Even a new theory as to the historicity of the Shroud effected only a momentary hesitation in the slowly solidifying opposition. It was asserted by a Father Chamard that the Shroud had been brought to France from Constantinople, after the last Crusade of 1204, by Othon de la Roche, a French knight. De la Roche had given it to the cathedral of Besançon, Chamard claimed, where it had remained until it was stolen during a fire. Subsequently it passed through the hands of the King of France and finally into the possession of Geoffrey de Charny. This theory, however, rested on shaky tradition and involuted documentary sources. It did not gain complete acceptance even among the relic's supporters.

The noise of the disagreement grew fainter as the years passed. All efforts to gain access to the Shroud failed, although by 1910, according to Vignon, only the King of Italy stood in the way. Discouraged and perhaps disgusted, Vignon turned back to biology and began important work, among other things, as a pioneer in the art of natural camouflage. He served briefly at the front in the First World War as a lieutenant and afterwards began teaching at the *Institut Catholique*. Pictures of the Shroud hung in his house, but his mind, once so full of the relic, drifted farther and farther from the topic, engrossed in more immediate matters. In 1920 Yves Delage died and three years later Ulysse Chevalier followed him. As the twenties bloomed and faded, it was only in his heart that Paul Vignon still carried a small hope that some day he would look on the cloth with his own eyes.

9

INTERLUDE:

THE LONG ARM OF FATHER THURSTON

A surprising fact soon grips the attention of anyone tracing the story of the Turin enigma: the English language has comparatively little to offer on the subject. Only nine books, a dozen pamphlets and fewer than sixty magazine articles are available. By contrast, there are hundreds of books and thousands of articles in French and Italian. This situation was seen as something of a mystery. Surely the cloth, even with its controverted authenticity, held as much interest for English-speaking Christians as it did for those of other nationalities. Why such a discrepancy?

The reason, it appears, can be assigned to the role played

by one man—the Rev. Herbert Thurston, an English Jesuit. It was his condemnation of the relic, voiced soon after Delage's lecture, that muted and almost stifled the controversy in the English-speaking world. Although he added little that was really original to the arguments against the cloth, his position in the story for readers of English was a crucial one.

Until his death in 1939, this priest, a scholar of vast erudition, held a uniquely powerful sway in the field of church history. Capable of enormous industry, he was an odd combination of balanced intellectual reserve, and downright pugnacity. Many of his opinions embroiled him in public argument, often with the traditionalists of his own church. But so exact and sure was his grasp of his materials that he rarely, if ever, was forced to recant.

In his small room in the Jesuit house at Farm Street, London—a picturesque jumble of books, correspondence, magazines, galley-proofs and manuscripts—he produced an incredible amount and variety of writings. The approximately 400 articles to his credit ranged over such topics as the English birthrate, Shakespeare's religion, clerical scandals, spiritualism, church bells, Joan of Arc, Christian Science, witchcraft, Bernadette of Lourdes, poltergeists and divining rods. The bulk of his writing concerned ecclesiastical history but he had a decided penchant for the unusual. His last article, posthumously published, was entitled "Pacts with the Devil." He was especially noted as an implacable foe of spurious history and uncertain relics.

His reputation spread far beyond the normal confines of his faith. The public knew him through a number of rousing controversies with such luminaries as Sir H. Rider Haggard and Sir Arthur Conan Doyle. Once he displayed dazzling virtuosity in answering a challenge flung at him by the historian Coulton.

In evaluating the works of another writer, Thurston had claimed, rather rashly, that ten mistakes probably could be dug out of any ten consecutive pages. Coulton resurrected the statement thirty-three years after it was made and defied Thurston to do it. The pages were chosen, at random, by a disinterested party with all the formality of a trial at arms. Within a month, Thurston exposed and lengthily proved some *fifteen* errors!

For English readers, his entry into the Turin dispute began with a letter to *The Times*: "Will you allow me to point out," he inquired, "that before we can profitably discuss the value of Dr. Vignon's scientific explanation of the marks on the Holy Shroud a serious difficulty of quite another order has to be cleared up?" He recalled the work of Chevalier concerning the charge of Bishop d'Arcis and noted that Chevalier was a scholar of distinction. In a long contribution to *The Month*, a Jesuit periodical for which he was a staff writer, he expanded on the theme and supplied a translation of the whole Latin memorandum in which d'Arcis had levelled his accusation of forgery.

His conclusion was a model of judicious evaluation, quite unlike the raucous posturings that had too often split the air in France and Italy:

There are many minor points that might be urged, but what has been said seems to me sufficient to settle the question, if anything can settle it. Of course, all historical evidence is to some extent relative. What we treat as conclusive in discussing the events of the fourteenth century, would not perhaps be sufficient to convict a prisoner on trial for his life in a modern court of law. None the less, the case is here so strong that however plausible M. Vignon's scientific hypothesis may seem, the probability of an error in the verdict of history must be accounted, it seems to me, as almost infinitesimal.

Although he was convinced of the falsity of the relic, he did not shy away from the scientific aspects of the problem. He dealt with it in the next issue of *The Month*. "Who could have dreamed," he asked wonderingly, "that the Shroud of Turin . . . should find vindicators even in the Academy of Sciences itself, and that agnostic professors of the Sorbonne should venerate a relic of the Passion which Jesuits and Monsignori had repudiated?" Few of Vignon's attackers, he thought, had treated him or his arguments fairly. Some had been seriously discourteous and others had welcomed all theories in opposition, blandly glossing over the mutual in-consistencies. The central point at issue, he felt, was whether the image was really a negative, in the sense Vignon intended.

> The most fundamental point is undoubtedly the question of the so-called negative image. I think the term is confusing and to some extent question-begging, but if we understand by *negative* simply a picture in which the normal lights and shadows are reversed, I do not see how it can be disputed that in its present state the image, or more accurately the two images, on the shroud are negatives . . . but in con-ceding that the image is now a negative, it must not be inferred that I am surrendering the whole position. Sup-posing that it were a question of a delicate portrait on linen in simple black and white, and supposing also that the "negative" characteristics had been observed from the beginning, or at any rate before the fire, I for one should admit the validity of M. Vignon's conclusion that the image seen thereon could hardly have been painted by the hand

of man. Unfortunately, however, for his theory, these conditions are by no means verified.

Eyewitness accounts, Thurston contended, proved that the image was not in simple black and white, but in a yellowish colour, "the very tint which was most likely to lead to photographic complications." Aware of the force of Vignon's contention that the flimsy material of the relic would not have retained the heavy pigmentation of oil paints, he suggested that the portrait might have been executed in water colours. Moreover, he said, the whole subject of medieval colouring materials was hopelessly obscure. Vegetable tinctures or even dyes might have been used and it was impossible to guess what liquids were employed to dilute or fix them.

He reasoned:

It appears to me quite conceivable that the figure of Our Lord may have originally been painted in two different yellows, a bright glazed yellow for the lights and a brownish yellow for the shadows. What chemist would be bold enough to affirm that under the action of time and of intense heat the two yellows may have behaved very differently, the bright yellow blackening, the brown yellow fading? We cannot possibly dogmatize about the behaviour of colouring matters the nature of which is unknown to us.

The Shroud of Turin, Thurston decided, had probably originated as a devotional aid in the complicated Easter rites of the Middle Ages. (In this, of course, he was consciously rejecting d'Arcis' charge of deliberate fraud.) From the idea he drew some interesting suppositions:

There was probably a certain demand for such cloths . . . a monk who had chanced to give satisfaction by painting a human figure on the shroud with some skill, would be likely to receive many other commissions and to have abundant opportunities of improving on his first rude efforts. I see therefore no violent improbability that such an artist may have studied the nude figure and the impressions left by the body of a man lying supine.

A painter of such devotional shrouds, he theorized, would in time undoubtedly come to see that he should paint not a picture of a man, but an image as if it had been made by contact. In this way, without the artist intending it, there would develop the negativity of the imprint. Thus, for Thurston, the true solution was either an inversion of colours or a painting based on a live model.

His two articles appeared in *The Month* for January and February of 1903. Thereafter, for more than twenty years, no one writing in English took issue with him. The relic was forgotten outside of continental Europe. Even impartial observers have regretted this period of silence, since it was clear that the problem had not been settled, if for no other reason than that the cloth itself had not been examined. The situation bears a disquieting resemblance to the twenty-year eclipse of the Altamira cave-paintings after their rejection by a Lisbon congress of antiquarians. Altamira was eventually vindicated, but a generation of research had been lost even though the paintings, unlike the Shroud, were freely available for study.

In 1912, Thurston himself revived memories of the Shroud with his contribution to the *Catholic Encyclopedia*, but in so doing only condemned it anew under semi-official auspices.

It was the Rev. P. A. Beecher of Ireland, who broke the thralldom. He accused the brilliant Jesuit of misleading not only the learned but the public as well, by his article in the encyclopedia. "He has not only denied its authenticity, but has conveyed the impression that the arguments on the opposite side are scarcely worth considering." It was Beecher's claim that the Shroud could not be a painting because the artistic ability to make it did not exist in the Middle Ages. Even the great Giotto, who flourished at that period, couldn't produce an entirely natural human face, argued Beecher. If Giotto couldn't do it then no one else at the time could, for Giotto was the giant of his era, As for Thurston's water-colour theory, which kind did he mean, Beecher wanted to know— the ancient or the modern? If the ancient, he was again confronted by excessive pigmentation; if the modern, he was caught in an anachronism, since present-day water-colour techniques were not developed until the eighteenth century.

Beecher summed up:

> Father Thurston's position is virtually this: at a time when, in France, painting was practically non-existent, an artist arose who proved himself greater than Giotto and yet managed to remain nameless, who held the secret which, if divulged, would have advanced painting by some two hundred years . . . who used water colours centuries before water-colouring became known to others, and who at the same time, and for some peculiar whim, and through a process unknown until the invention of photography, worked through the medium of a negative, so that no one might ever know what he had done.

In 1928, Beecher produced a book of some 200 pages, in which he surveyed the whole question. The work was subtitled *A Reply to the Rev. Herbert Thurston S.J.* and it concentrated largely on reconstructing the historical record of the relic all the way back to Calvary. Like all such efforts, however, the attempt was a demonstration of possibilities, rather than proof of an uninterrupted provenance, and was seen as such even by the relic's advocates. The book was an outspoken frontal attack and Beecher thoughtfully apologized for its aggressive tone. But, he pointed out, he was fighting a quarter of a century of settled opinion and "we must shout to be heard!"

Beecher's shouting, however, could not pierce the solid wall of opposition, or more accurately, move the dead weight of indifference that had formed like an encrustation. Thurston held the field. It was not until 1934 that anyone writing in English again ventured a full-scale defence of the Shroud. But by that time the relic had succeeded, at last, in riveting men's attention.

Part Three

10

1931: THE CAMERA AGAIN

The skies over Turin were disappointingly sombre on May 3rd, 1931. They held the look of rain. In spite of the threat, since early morning immense crowds had been surging through the streets towards the Cathedral of St. John. In a few hours the Holy Shroud would be taken from its silver casket and raised up once more in the gilded frame. The new Exposition was being held to celebrate the marriage of the King's son, Crown Prince Umberto; love had accomplished what thirty years of entreaty could not.

The city was already overwhelmed by visitors but every train brought thousands more. The response of the devout, from all over Europe, had the feel of a spontaneous reaffirmation of faith in the relic after a third of a century of partial rejection. Perhaps, too, there was something of wishful striving—Christian piety did not want to be deprived of its most glorious link with the Redemption.

Permission to make new pictures was granted unhesitatingly

by the King, and the Exposition Committee, under Maurillio Cardinal Fossati, moved with care in its selection of a photographer. In the time that had passed since Pia took the first picture, the art had made huge strides. Lenses, shutter speeds, plate sensitivity, filters and developing procedures had been improved, refined and specialized. Cardinal Fossati, aware of the importance of technical perfection, wanted a man of the highest professional standing, as well as one with a suitable background of responsibility. The choice fell on Giuseppe Enrie of Turin. A long-time professional, Enrie had been editor of *Vita Fotografica Italiana*, and had served as president of a photographic society. At the time of his selection, he ran his own highly successful studio. A man of strong convictions and professional pride, he would need these very qualities for the successful completion of his work.

At a meeting with the Cardinal, Enrie outlined his plans. He would take a number of views of the whole Shroud; at least one of these would be made in three sections on three separate plates. The face, as the most important element on the cloth, would be shot in various sizes, once in a size corresponding to the original. To satisfy the scholarly requests that arrived with almost every mail, he would photograph some of the details, such as the blood on the wrist. This would also serve as an enlargement of the fabric, allowing experts to study the material itself for the first time. For this task, he would use an apparatus that enlarged the subject seven times directly on to the plate. Subsequent superficial blow-ups from these enlargements would render the smallest items clear. But it was absolutely essential, Enrie stressed, that the pictures be made without the obstruction of glass. The Shroud must be removed from its frame. The Cardinal, pleased with Enrie's grasp of the assignment, nodded agreement.

Like Pia before him, however, Enrie's work was to be
made doubly difficult by the ponderous formalities. At first,
he was given only two hours in which to operate. And the
hordes of people besieging the cathedral—many of them
returning again and again—were present from daybreak till
dark. Even then the pace didn't slow. In addition to a
nocturnal guard of honour, there was always a large cluster
of those who had obtained special permission to spend the
night. A continual flow of priests eddied around the
altar, each hoping to celebrate Mass in front of the cloth. Only
a fraction ever gained the privilege, even though the chain
of Masses began well before dawn. Throughout the twenty
days of the Exposition the cathedral would never be
empty.

A light rain finally began to fall by afternoon on the third.
In the Royal Chapel, Cardinal Fossati lifted the relic from its
case, severed the bindings and helped to unroll it on the long
table. After the ceremonial kissing by the House of Savoy and
the assembled prelates, it was taken into the cathedral, fixed to
its backing and placed in the frame. As the last word of the
Cardinal's sermon echoed in the silence, the cathedral bells
began tolling and the sound was picked up by one church after
another until the whole city resounded with the erratic
symphony.

All day a steady stream of men and women, religious and
laity, poured into the Plaza of St. John and through the big
wooden doors. At 10:30 P.M., the entrance guards moved to
halt the traffic. Cries of protest went up, but the doors were
shut. The next two hours belonged to Enrie and his camera.
In the sacristy darkroom he had set up beforehand, the photographer readied his equipment. With him, as advisers, were
two men who had spent nearly half their lives waiting for this

moment: Secondo Pia, now seventy-five, and Paul Vignon, ten years younger.

By 11 p.m. the long board to which the relic was affixed had been taken from the high frame and propped at the foot of the altar. The crowd of witnesses in the sanctuary surged forward for a closer look; here and there some better-prepared scholars peered through magnifying glasses, their faces only inches from the cloth. Whenever a picture was not being taken, they pushed forward again. Curbing his own impatience, Enrie would allow them long moments of inspection.

While Cardinal Fossati smoothed out the slight wrinkles that had developed in the cloth, Enrie set up his two cameras and adjusted the lighting. At Enrie's request, the Cardinal moved the Shroud this way and that while the camera sought perfect focus.

Enrie made his first exposure, as a control, with the lens focused on the head and upper torso. In the sacristy darkroom, as he placed the plate in the bath, Pia and Vignon hovered over his shoulder, watching anxiously for the first murky forms to take shape. Then, with sudden clarity, there appeared under the developer the same face Pia had seen thirty-three years before, only in infinitely more meticulous detail. The old photographer felt a wave of relief; the pictures would soon be before the eyes of the world, and there would be no more unfair charges of dishonesty.

A few seconds later the picture was in the hands of the Cardinal. Afterwards, Enrie recalled: "I will remember as one of the most beautiful moments of my life, certainly the most moving of my career, the instant in which I submitted my perfect plate to the avid look of the Archbishop and that select whole group of people."

By 12:30 he had exposed six more plates, using three settings and distances, and the second camera. All of these showed the entire Shroud; he had not yet taken any of the important details so eagerly desired by scholars. But his time was up and the priests waiting to begin Mass milled around impatiently. Enrie, not sure he would be permitted to return another day or that the cloth would again be removed from its case, stuck to his post. He moved a camera up closer, applied a special lens, trained it on the face of the image, and opened the shutter. But with the exposure only half complete, the camera was accidentally jarred. It was then after one o'clock and Enrie realized he would have to give up.

While waiting for permission to have the relic taken out again—something only the King could decide—Enrie set up a large tripod and a ladder and on the evening of the 21st photographed the Shroud, in its glass-fronted frame, in three sections.

The next day the permission was granted and in the evening Enrie took three pictures of the face, one in life size, a picture of the shoulders and back, and a sevenfold enlargement of the wound in the wrist. The shot of the wrist wound was also intended as a picture of the fabric itself.

A delegation of five professional photographers, invited by Enrie, now studied all the plates and compared them with the relic. An affidavit was drawn up stating:

1st. That the negative photographic plates are absolutely free from any indication of retouching or other artifice, for which reason the same retains the genuine photographic expression of the Holy Cloth reproduced;

2nd. That, from diligent and accurate comparison of the photographic prints direct with the original, the most faithful reproduction and irreproachable workmanship has been established.

With that, Enrie's task was finished, but his connection with the Shroud was only beginning. Until his death in 1962, he handled the world-wide dispersal of the new pictures in answer to an ever-growing demand. In this work he encountered a whim that harked back to the early naïve notions about pictures of the Shroud. A picture made directly from the original plates, he found, was prized by the public above one made from secondary plates, although there existed no visual difference between the two. The light rays that had etched the original, it was felt, had actually touched the cloth, providing a closer, if somewhat sentimental, connection with the relic and the Man who had left His image on it.

It would be some time before opinions emerged from the flurry of research that now began, but a number of things became apparent even before the end of the Exposition.

It could be seen at a glance that the figure of the body, and especially the face, was even more perfectly formed than was evident in the old picture. The accuracy of the negative values was absolute. The majestic expression of the face was more pronounced and powerful. Nowhere in the stains that formed the image were there any outlines. Nor could strokes or brushmarks be picked out. No other known method of manual application of colour, such as dottings, could be seen. The unmarked parts of the cloth *within* the area of the image were perfectly free of stains of any kind; they reproduced the faded tone of the rest of the cloth.

But it was in the sevenfold enlargement of the wrist area that the scholars found the most important, unassailable new fact: *the individual threads* of the material could be seen clearly, as well as the depressions between them, and there wasn't even a trace of colouring matter. Pigmentation inevitably would have filled the depressions and resulted in massed patches under which the threads would be united and hidden. Yet each thread retained its separate and individual existence. The image was an ineffably delicate suffusion of discoloration in the threads.

This same picture yielded other information that would soon after lead to a separate branch of study. Textile experts identified the fabric as pure flax, woven from coarse, rough-fibred, handspun yarn. The irregular lines and imperfections in the weave indicated a hand-made product. One expert claimed he could even identify the degree of refinement of the two types of threads; they corresponded, he said, to #50 and #70 of present-day English flax count. The pattern was easily identified as herringbone (twill). The weave, in textile terms, was 3 to 1, broken at intervals with a forty-thread stripe.

It was quickly—and happily—realized, that the cloth itself presented no obstacle to authenticity. Similar designs in linen were still preserved from a time well before Christ in the East. On the other hand, Western Europe did not use the twill weave until much later than the fourteenth century. It was with some pardonable degree of relish that this last point was made by the cloth's adherents. History had at last started to turn in their favour.

As Turin emptied of its two million visitors after the last day of the Exposition, the scholars departed armed with copies of the new pictures. A new phase in the study of the relic was about to dawn, one in which scientists would pile up an impressive body of evidence in the relic's favour while opponents would hold fast to the documentary charge of forgery. In time, this line of demaraction would become fairly well defined as scientist vs. historian, with a sub-conflict on the biblical level.

At least, it was agreed, this time the controversy was here to stay. There could be no fading of interest, no turning back, until the final solution was reached.

11

PIERRE BARBET:
A SURGEON EXPERIMENTS

In a Paris apartment, one evening in 1932, Dr. Pierre Barbet was excited as he sat down to dinner with his family. "The thumb turned inward," he exclaimed, demonstrating with his hand, "inward on the palm! When the nail went through the wrist—poof! there it was, the thumb completely hidden!" The children listened respectfully and went on eating. Such talk from their father had become a regular part of the evening meal. They knew he had lately taken an interest in the Holy Shroud, but were unaware he had just announced a dramatic occurrence in the resurgent study of the relic.

The man who now comes on stage could not have fitted his role more perfectly if he had been hand-picked; nor could his appearance have been better timed. In ability, background and temperament, he was the ideal investigator to work on the new pictures.

A surgeon, Barbet had also been a teacher of anatomy, living for thirteen years, as he expressed it, in close contact with corpses. He was active in the Society of St. Luke, a French group that studied medical questions touching on religion and faith. Intensely religious himself, he was a daily communicant and always knelt on the ground at the rear of the church, muttering his prayers in Greek.

As a linguist he was known for his translation of the poems of the Italian Jacopone Da Todi. His more intellectual countrymen ranked him with the leading Dante scholars. A voracious reader, with an extremely precise mind, he made marginal notes in almost every book he read—including detective stories. He simply could not pass a doubtful statement in silence. For relaxation he played the violin and until his later years he swam, played tennis and went riding. When he gave up sport, his short solid body began to take on weight; sport had been a means of combating corpulence.

He possessed great powers of concentration and endurance as a surgeon. Once during the Second World War, he stood at an operating table for eighteen consecutive hours, repairing one mangled body after another. At the Hospital of St. Joseph, where he was head surgeon for thirty-five years, he had acquired a reputation for speed—thirty operations a week were nothing unusual for him. When his colleagues expressed admiration for such facility, however, he would reply, as if to ward off any imputation of carelessness: "I do not operate quickly. I merely eliminate wasted motion."

Born in 1883, Barbet was married to the daughter of a Vatican engineer in 1910. The death of his wife seventeen years later cast a pall over his spirit that never lifted. It was her loss that plunged him into religion and the distracting world of the intellect. Long afterwards, his children—five girls and one boy—recalled the austere life that descended on them without the softening presence of their mother.

Like so many others, Barbet's connection with the Shroud began accidentally, almost as a matter of academic interest. In 1931, while he was presiding over a conference of medical students, a friend, a Father d'Armailhac, showed him Enrie's pictures and asked him if he would undertake a short anatomical study of the figures. More to oblige a friend than because of any deep interest in the relic, Barbet consented. Before he finished he had instituted an entirely new approach to the problem and composed one of the most movingly graphic accounts of the Passion ever written.

His principal task was to check the wounds on the Shroud against anatomical reality, and it was the wrist that attracted him first. The location didn't bother him since he knew that the traditional view of the nail having been in the palm was just a layman's misconception. To anatomists, the hand was always made up of fingers, palm and wrist. But exactly *where* in the wrist had the nail been driven through? The bony structure at this point was a complex unit, each of its parts known, named and bearing a constant relation to the others. It did not seem possible that a nail could have gone through this compact mass without smashing one or more of the bones, and Barbet knew that this possibility was inadmissible to a Christian. Even by smashing the bones, the nail might not have been able to penetrate.

Careful measurements on the enlargements confirmed that the wound had been inflicted just above the fleshy ridge of the upper palm, in a spot corresponding to the chief bending fold of the wrist. Through comparison Barbet located it at the edge of the transverse carpal ligament. He frowned as he studied his charts. There seemed no way for even a small nail to go through here.

His position as a surgeon and anatomist at one of the great hospitals of Paris afforded him unique opportunities for experimental work on cadavers and amputated limbs. Now, faced with the anomaly of the wrist wound, he decided that only such direct experiment would suffice. Taking a newly-amputated arm—which he himself had removed from a patient shortly before—he drove a large nail through the wrist at the point where his measurements indicated. When the nail passed through the soft parts and hit the bones, the point began to slide a little upwards in spite of Barbet's firm grip on it. Then, after one or two more blows, the nail suddenly tore through the wrist and emerged at the back of the hand—in exactly the same spot as shown on the relic. It had found some totally unsuspected anatomical passage-way. But it was not this fact that made the surgeon gape in surprise; it was the thumb. Jerking spontaneously as the spike cut its way through the flesh, the thumb had jammed itself inward on the palm. Instinctively Barbet knew he had found the answer to another of those supposed "errors" so many had pointed out on the relic; the stain image of the hands—crossed, palms downward —showed no sign of thumbs.

Minutes later, his scalpel had bared the technical reasons for both the ease of the nail's penetration and the movement of the thumb. A tiny free space among the middle bones had been forcibly widened by the nail to form an unobstructed passage. This very spot had been labelled by French anatomists as the Space of Destot and it had long been known because of the part it played in wrist dislocation. But it had not been considered by Barbet, or anyone else, as a possibility because it was little more than a miniscule depression at the juncture of four bones. Now he could see that the nail had enlarged it just enough to permit entry. "Is it possible," he asked later, "that trained executioners would not have known by experience of this ideal spot for crucifying the hands?"

The reason for the unexpected thumb spasm was also quickly uncovered and it added a shudder-provoking bit of realism to the otherwise skimpy account of the crucifixion ordeal. The median nerve of the wrist had been damaged by Barbet's nail and this mechanical stimulation activated the short flexor muscles controlling the thumb. "Could a forger have imagined *this*?" the surgeon wondered. A sensitive man as well as a precise one, he subsequently explained the physical significance of this brutal interference with the median nerve in a living body:

> The median nerves are not merely the motor nerves, they are also the great sensory nerves. When they are injured and stretched out on the nails in those extended arms, like the strings of a violin on their bridge, they must have caused the most horrible pain. Those who have seen, during the war, something of the wounds of the nervous trunks, know that it is one of the worst tortures imaginable. So bad is it that its prolongation would not be compatible with life without some sort of suspension of the normal functions. This most frequently takes the form of a fainting fit. Now Our Saviour . . . went on living and speaking . . . for about three hours!

Afterwards, Barbet repeated the experiment a dozen times. Though he moved the nail all around the middle of the bending fold, it always slipped into the same space, seeking the line of least resistance.

It was the strange shape of the bloodstain on the wrist that led him into some further discoveries that later would enable him to give powerful effect to his word-picture of the Passion. He noted that there seemed to be two different streams flowing from the wound, each at a different angle. Plotting these geometrically with the axis of the arm he was able to prove that the flows had resulted from two alternating angles of the hands. He interpreted this to mean that the body on the cross had taken two positions: the first was a slumped posture in which the body hung from the nails at the wrists. But breathing while hanging this way was physically not possible, so it was necessary for the crucified to seek relief by raising himself and literally standing on the nails in his feet. Such torture could not be endured for long; the body would slump again and the slow asphyxiation would be resumed.

In the first position, Barbet computed from the blood flow, the arms formed an angle of sixty-five degrees with the vertical. In the second, one of sixty-eight or seventy degrees. He confirmed this to his own satisfaction by showing that if the arms had originally been nailed transversely, at an angle approximating ninety degrees with the vertical, then the body could not for anatomical reasons have descended below this angle of sixty-five degrees.

Of all the men who have studied the Shroud, Pierre Barbet was, in a way, the most fortunate. Just as he was concluding his work on the wrist, word reached Paris that the relic was again to be exposed, at the special request of Pope Pius XI.

Achille Ratti had risen steadily through the ecclesiastical ranks since the days when he shared Alpine dangers with Paul Vignon. From his position as Professor of Dogmatic Theology at the Great Seminary in Milan, he had been appointed to the

Ambrosian Library, where his scholarship, especially as a historian, attracted wide attention. In 1912 he was called to Rome to take charge of the Vatican Library. Ten years later he ascended the Throne of Peter as Pius XI. He had long before made up his mind about the Shroud of Turin, after a lengthy and persistent study of his own. As Pope he expressed his belief publicly, often distributing pictures of the Holy Face at his audiences. To Pia, Vignon and Barbet he gave private audiences, showing, as they reported, a masterful grasp of the scientific details.

With the approach of the nineteenth centenary of the Crucifixion, Pius XI declared 1933 a Holy Year and called for due observance throughout the Catholic world. He made a special request to the King of Italy for a new display of the Shroud and this was immediately granted. On September 24th, 1933, the relic was once more taken out and put on view in the cathedral. This exposition was for religious purposes and no photography was permitted, especially since it was scarcely two years since Enrie's work. During the exposition an even greater number of pilgrims attended than had responded in 1931.

Pierre Barbet was an avid observer for a few days towards the end of this session. Since his special interest centred on the five wounds, he was most concerned with the marks of blood on the cloth. In the well-lighted sanctuary of St. John's' Cathedral, he stood at the foot of the altar and strained for a close look at the image and the blood. But he could pick out no significant new factors. The distance was too great and the lighting, while strong, was not correctly angled to bring out nuances of colour and contour. To Barbet, both the image and the blood on it seemed to be of a brownish tint, with the blood simply darker than the rest.

But on October 15th, closing day, he was unexpectedly given an opportunity to view the relic in daylight from a distance of less than a yard. The experience overwhelmed him and it was probably at this moment that he changed from detached investigator to fervent partisan. In the work that he did afterwards he still used scientific exactitude but he was less concerned with proving authenticity. Now it became a matter of reconstructing the Passion of the Lord in its smallest detail.

Barbet's opportunity came in late afternoon. As was usual on the day when the relic was to be returned to its casket, a huge crowd filled the Plaza of St. John; the people had no expectation of getting inside for the terminal functions and merely wanted to be present during the last moments. As the sun dipped behind the houses opposite the cathedral a whisper sped through the crowd: Cardinal Fossati had decided to take the relic out on to the broad terrace at the top of the steps so that those outside might have a final chance to see it. Barbet hurried outdoors ahead of the slowly moving procession that carried the cloth still extended on its backing. He posted himself at the edge of the terrace. The bright but diffused light was ideal. The procession emerged through the big double doors and out to the terrace, Cardinal Fossati in his heavy gold cope and tall, pointed mitre leading the way. An order was murmured and the procession stopped. The long cloth was allowed to rest on its edge on the top step. Barbet had chosen his spot well; the relic was directly in front of him.

I suddenly experienced one of the most powerful emotions of my life. For without expecting it, I saw that all the images of the wounds were of a colour quite different from that of the rest of the body; and this colour was that of dried blood which had sunk into the stuff. There was, thus, more than the brown stains on the shroud reproducing the outline of the corpse. The blood itself had coloured the stuff by direct contact . . . It is difficult for one unversed in painting to define the exact colour, but the foundation was red (mauve carmine, said M. Vignon, who had a fine sense of colour) diluted more or less according to the wounds; it was the strongest at the side, at the head, the hands and the feet; it was paler but nevertheless fully visible in the innumerable marks of the scourging . . . but a surgeon could understand, with no possibility of doubt, that it was the blood which had sunk into the linen, and this blood was the Blood of Christ!

Overcome, Barbet sank to his knees in the steps of the cathedral and bowed his head.

Later, when he was criticized for what appeared to be unscientific enthusiasm, he replied that he understood the need for chemical and physical tests that might detect such things as haemoglobin or its derivatives. But, he added, he had perceived visual certainties in those few moments in front of the cathedral, elements that were plain even in the photographs, such as the characteristic separation of fibrin and serum and the concavity of the centres. His sudden descryal of the reddish-carmine colouring of the spots had given him moral certainty of the genuineness of the blood. "I had recognized them just as one recognizes the image of a familiar face."

Back in Paris, Barbet renewed his experiments.

Only the bloody sole of the right foot had left an imprint on the cloth, but the cramped attitude of the legs seemed to indicate that one foot had been crossed over the other and the feet fixed to the cross with one nail. Tradition, the surgeon knew, supported a number of views on the nailing of the feet. Artists almost always depicted the right foot crossed over the left and some early commentators claimed that each foot had been nailed separately. To Barbet, though, as well as to Shroud students before him, the evidence of the Shroud was in favour of one nail and a crossing of the feet, the left over the right.

A concavity was traceable in the right sole, corresponding to the arch of the foot. There were vague imprints of toes, slightly separated each from the other, as though the man they belonged to had never worn a shoe. In the centre of the blood-stains on the ball of the foot Barbet picked out a darker, rectangular patch that seemed to be the source of the meander-ing streams. Here the point of the nail had emerged, he theorized.

But where had the nail entered? And again, did the location fit in with anatomical truth?

Measurements allowed him only to approximate the posi-tion of the wounds; the prints were too indefinite for greater precision. The rectangular stain appeared to fall just in front of ''Lisfranc's Spaceline'' between the second and third toes. There was no difficulty here, as a short experiment on a cadaver showed. The nail easily went in and poked through the sole at just the spot indicated by the relic.

The lance thrust into the side of the dead Christ had always been a favourite topic of biblical commentators and mystics, and it was to this that Barbet turned next. The high interest in this particular wound was derived primarily from St. John's eye-witness statement: ''One of the soldiers with a lance opened His side, and immediately there came out blood and water.'' Through the centuries, writers had mulled over those words, drawing from them involved symbolic meanings centring on Christ's role as the Redeemer. They all agreed that the thing must really have happened, since the Evangelist reported it. But they preferred to look on the blood and water as miraculous. Neither blood nor water could come from a corpse, they insisted. After death, blood coagulated in the body and could not flow. The water was even less understandable; dead bodies did not exude water of any kind. There was none present. The only answer was a miracle allowed by the dying Jesus as one last act of love. This idea was widespread even in the twentieth century.

As a doctor, however, Barbet knew that blood did *not* coagulate in a corpse. It remained fluid for some time. Concerning the water, he had the glimmering of an idea.

To fix the true position of the wound he made two series of complicated anatomical measurements. The first began with the pronounced impression of the pectoral (chest) muscles and their nipples. The second started at the clearly marked substernal hollow. The convergence of guidelines from these two measurements told him that the wound lay between the fifth and sixth ribs, about six inches from the mesial line. From this point on a man's side, the right auricle of the heart was less than four inches away and in a corpse it was always filled with liquid blood.

Taking a needle with a syringe attached, he inserted it into a cadaver, just above the sixth rib. At a depth of about four inches the needle entered the right auricle. Barbet applied suction and the tube filled with blood.

He repeated the experiment, this time inserting the needle very slowly. When he felt the tip puncture the pericardial sac (a thin membrane enclosing the heart) he stopped and squeezed the little rubber ball. Immediately the tube filled with a clear, watery serum. Then he pushed the needle on into the right auricle again and blood flowed in, mingling with the serum. There, he told himself, was St. John's "water"—the pericardial fluid. The Evangelist had called it water because it looked like water. Even medical science referred to it as the "hydropericardium"—water contained in the pericardium.

He tried the experiment again, this time with a knife, inserting it slowly. The watery fluid flowed down the blade, followed by blood. But the lance thrust on Calvary could not have been such a deliberate, controlled stroke. It must have been delivered with vigour. Taking his knife again he shoved it into the cadaver as if it were the spear of a Roman legionary. Blood poured out, and around the edges Barbet could see the clear pericardial fluid. St. John had told the exact truth, but it had taken twenty centuries to vindicate him.

During the years that followed these early experiments, Barbet engaged in an even more intense investigation, branching into the fields of scripture and archaeology, as well as medicine, searching always for evidence to uphold the Shroud. To him the most insignificant detail connected with the Passion grew to have an infinite value. He carefully pieced together every scrap of information he could find about the descent from the cross, the carrying of the body to the tomb, and the actual burial. At times the subject engrossed his attention almost to the point where he could think of nothing else. Finally from this mass of information he produced a unique document on the Crucifixion—a medical description of Christ's sufferings. It appeared in 1940 as *The Corporal Passion of Jesus Christ*.

A powerful combination of emotional insights and simplified medical description, *The Corporal Passion* soon became widely known in France and the neighbouring countries as a basis for

Easter Week sermons. In some churches, seminaries and monasteries it replaced the usual comtemplative fare, often being read aloud in its entirety. Today it is a minor classic, and undoubtedly would have gained even greater fame if it had not been based largely on information derived from the Shroud. The controversial relic has managed to wrap Barbet's masterpiece in its own cloudy prison.

Focusing on the mental as well as the physical tortures of the Messiah, *The Corporal Passion* begins with a description of the bloody sweat (a rupture of the subcutaneous capillaries), goes on to a circumstantial account of the buffeting; the scourging; carrying of the cross; the stripping of the clothes ("Have you ever removed the first dressing which has been on a large bruised wound, and has dried on it?"); the horrible nailing of the hands and feet; the indescribable pains of the lingering hours on the cross; and the merciful death (asphyxiation after a progressive tetanization). No one who reads this amazing work forgets it. Barbet admitted that he wrote it "not without tears."

In the end, this intimate knowledge of Christ's sufferings lay like a livid scar in his imagination. "I can assure you of a dreadful thing," he wrote, "I have reached the point when I no longer dare to think of them. No doubt this is cowardice, but I hold that one must either have heroic virtue or else fail to understand; that one must either be a saint or else irresponsible, in order to do the Way of the Cross. I no longer can."

One incident from the twenty years of his studies was reported by Barbet as his supreme moment of reward. It is equally apt as a momentary illumination of the ultimate attraction so many men have felt for the relic of Turin.

When he was readying his work on the cloth for the press, Barbet wanted an objective opinion from an unbiased, scientific observer. For this purpose he could think of no one more suitable than an old friend, Professor Hovelacque of the *Ecole Pratique*, an anatomist and a man of iron honesty, but an unbeliever in religion. Hovelacque listened closely as the surgeon read his work, agreeing to the experiments and conclusions with a growing enthusiasm. At the finish, Hovelacque sat silent for a few moments. Then he looked up at Barbet, spread his hands and whispered "But then, my friend . . . Jesus Christ *did* rise again!"

12

THE DEEPENING PROBE

Though he was nearing seventy, Paul Vignon plunged once more into the study of the relic with the same enthusiasm he had shown in his thirties. By now the tacitly acknowledged leader in Shroud circles, his suggestion for organizing a mass scientific attack on the remaining problems was quickly taken up. A commission of experts was formed, with main divisions in France and Italy. Unable to gain access to the cloth itself, they concentrated enormous efforts on interpreting the details in the photographs and in unravelling the biblical and historical tangle.

By the start of the Second World War the Shroud had been studied more closely than in all its previous history. So widespread did interest in it become, and so complex the nature of the investigation, that it assumed the stature of a separate discipline and was given a name, *sindonology* (*sindon* meaning shroud). In those pre-war years, at least fifty scholars—

predominantly Italian, but including men in France, Germany, Spain, Czechoslovakia, England, Ireland and America— published decisions in favour of authenticity. During the same time the active opposition numbered about half a dozen—all of them historians or exegetes. This growing volume of approval was due to the interest shown by doctors, scientists and medical men generally. Thus the controversy was extended along the lines that, broadly speaking, prevail today: scientist vs. historian.

Almost all the scientists who have studied the Shroud have declared that it could not be the work of a man. The opponents do not attempt to meet the scientific arguments, but affirm that history and the Gospels are against the relic. To date no specific scientific objection has ever been recorded against the cloth. Other branches of learning have also lent support to authenticity. One of the more interesting of these was by Henri Terguem, a Protestant lawyer of Dunkerque. Applying the principles of legal evidence, he identified the body in the Shroud as that of Christ. His brochure was awarded the *Prix Montyon* by the French Academy.

But, rather fittingly, it was from Paul Vignon that the new sindonology received its most important impetus. Out of his background as a painter, he evolved an idea that lighted the dark years of the Shroud's primitive existence. First presented in 1938, his brilliant "Iconographic Theory" purported to show that the relic of Turin, with its imprint, was known and reverenced as far back as the fifth century.

The theory had its beginnings in a fact already known to historians of art. The physical appearance of Christ in paintings, sculptures and carvings can be rather sharply divided into two periods, with the line of separation running through the fourth century. In the first period—from the evidence of the catacomb pictures and some early Christian sarcophagi—Christ is depicted as a beardless youth with an oval face exuding the clarity of innocence. The stress is on His divinity; His humanity is lost in a gloss of shining naïveté. Nowhere, in all the art that has been preserved from the first 300 years after His death, is He seen any other way. Then, with the emergence of Christianity under Constantine, this obviously symbolic portrayal was discarded and pictures of Christ began to appear with the emphasis on His mature humanity—*always as the same set type.*

The face now was long and sharply profiled, the nose virile. The eyes were large and deep-set. The hair was parted in the middle and fell to the shoulders; the face carried a beard, often parted, and a moustache. The *fact* of this sudden and widespread change was known and it corresponded to the dawning curiosity that historians had noted as an element in the new freedom. What, people were asking in the bright days of Christianity's morning, did Christ *really* look like? But the underlying reasons for this total acceptance of a set type for Christ were never really searched for. Generally, it was supposed that the singular portrait was the fruit of tradition, or derived from some still more ancient original.

Yet historians knew that no reliable descriptions of the Messiah had ever been preserved. Not one of His contemporaries wrote down what He looked like. Early writers, in an effort to recapture the personage of Jesus, had to resort to theological speculation. But the whole subject was a twisting road leading backward into a jumble of legends.

For Vignon, however, the fact became an inspiration. *Might not the new type of Christ have been modelled on the relic?* If the Shroud had been hidden away under an official silence during the persecutions, and then brought out in Constantine's reign, it was possible—even probable—that the physiognomy of Christ would thereafter be based on the imprint. Undeniably, the portrait on the cloth bore the same features as the traditional Christ of the artists.

There must be some way to tie the two together, Vignon thought. If the Shroud was the progenitor of the traditional Christ, then something of the parent must have carried over into the offspring!

Eventually, after a long and minute comparison of the face on the cloth with hundreds of paintings, frescoes and mosaics, he found the answer. Certain peculiarities were evident in the Shroud—peculiarities that were really accidental imperfections in the image or the fabric itself, and that served no artistic purpose. Yet, he observed jubilantly, *these very oddities appeared again and again in a whole series of ancient art works, even though artistically they made no sense.* Surely, this could mean only one thing: ancient artists had taken their conception of a bearded, long-haired man from the image on the Shroud, and had included the anomalies because of a feeling that they were in some mysterious way connected with the earthly appearance of Jesus.

There were about twenty of these items in all; some very pronounced, some just strongly characteristic of the face on the cloth. Most arresting were such things as a small square set above the nose and open at the top, the result either of a defect in the weave or a unique, accidental stain. There was the distorted appearance of the nose, swollen at the bridge with the right nostril enlarged; the abnormal shading of the right cheek; a curved transverse stain that ran senselessly across the forehead.

Vignon was able to find no single art work in which all twenty or so of these peculiarities were present, but he didn't expect to. Different details could be traced in different works and some of the items appeared with more frequency than others. It was enough, he insisted, to discover even a few of them in any art work to establish a relationship with the Shroud. The peculiarities were distinctive of the relic and their existence could not be explained without it.

In the examples that Vignon provided, some of these oddities were reproduced with almost startling exactness; others appeared to be the artist's fumbling attempts to translate into living terms the grotesqueries of the negative imprint. This was only natural, explained Vignon, since these ancient artists had no understanding of the true nature of their model—its negativity. Moreover, some of the pictures were *copies of copies* and the strange little indicators had undergone some slight metamorphosis in the successive transitions.

The earliest example of a picture based on the relic was the Holy Face of Edessa, which could be dated in the fifth century. This portrait was one of the first *achiropoeton* (literally, *not made with hands*), and like the other such "miracle" pictures in early Eastern Christianity, it had a long and involved story of its own. Today it probably does not exist, although both Rome and Genoa claim to possess it. But there are copies available in which Vignon was able to trace the tell-tale signs of its dependence on the Shroud. Other examples he assigned to succeeding centuries and even placed the relic in Constantinople through comparison with the well-known Holy Face of Laon.

As with his earlier work, the new theory divided the critics. Some accepted it without reserve, calling it a magnificent new chapter in the history of art. The official bureau for the verification of the cures at Lourdes agreed that it filled in the emptiness of the lost millennium. But others rejected it in whole or in part and today it is still undergoing sifting and evaluation.

Some scholars have used the Iconographic Theory as a springboard for additions and variations. The German, Werner Bulst, and his colleagues held that all of the so-called "miraculous" pictures of antiquity, including the legend of Veronica's Veil, were derived from the relic of Turin, or from a knowledge of it in the primitive church.

Said Bulst:

In one point all of these legends surprisingly agree: the picture resulted from the *impression of the Face of Jesus on a cloth*. Often the cloth was called a *sudarium* or a sweat cloth. It was also called a *sindon* in the legends—the same word used by the Synoptics for the Shroud. In fact the word *sindon* is used in one of the oldest texts that makes mention of the picture of Edessa . . . [In another version] of the Edessa legend Jesus was stretched out to His full length on a linen cloth and an impression of His *whole figure* was left thereon . . . The question may well be raised whether so ancient and widespread a tradition about a cloth with the impress of Jesus might not have some historical point of contact . . .

The Iconographic Theory was Paul Vignon's last contribution to sindonology. When the Nazis overran France in 1940, he retired to d'Herbeys, where he wrote a philosophical synthesis of his life-long studies in science and religion. A granddaughter who stayed with him during those last years still remembers his erect figure striding down the long path to the road for his afternoon walk, garbed in a voluminous cloak and a broad-brimmed hat, with the little dog Dushka scampering after him. Though he was dying of cancer, he still said that walking was his health and he always cautioned any com-

panions on these strolls to maintain a good "mountain pace."
In his heart, thought his granddaughter, he was treading Alpine
peaks to the end. He died in the big old house at d'Herbeys
on October 17th, 1943. Over the deathbed hung a picture of
the face he had looked at, first in scepticism and then in
reverence, for nearly fifty years.

In 1939 the first Sindonological Congress was held in
Turin and was attended by many distinguished scholars. More
than twenty reports covered nearly the entire gamut of Shroud
research. It was the first definite sign that the study of the
relic had gone beyond the pioneer stage. It was also the first
time that a single relic had called forth such a gathering.
Today the Shroud of Turin, in terms of the number of people
involved, the time and effort given to it, and the size of its
literature, has become one of the two or three most cele-
brated "mysteries" of all time. In a popular, purely secular
sense, it ranks with the question of the Shakespeare authorship
and the legend of Atlantis. But just as those two famous
puzzles are known to the public only in their simplest forms,
so does the great body of facts connected with the Turin
enigma slumber undisturbed in professional journals and
scholarly books.

At present, the three main branches of sindonology are
scripture, history and science. In the first two categories, a
huge amount of energy had been expended by both sides but
it has become apparent that the result is a stalemate. Where
evidence depends on literary interpretation, based in its turn
on linguistics and psychology, there can never be a decision
that will satisfy everyone, certainly none that can carry an
over-riding conviction to the many.

The scriptural argument is simple enough on the surface,

but its roots are deep, twisted and too often spread out into thin filaments of conjecture. In the end, there is only this that can be said with certainty: No direct statement in any of the four Gospels disproves the authenticity of the Shroud. All argument, either for or against, rises from contradictory *interpretation*.

It is the same in the field of history. Why, ask the critics, is there no definite mention or description of the relic for more than its first thousand years? Why this "millennium of silence"? It isn't *altogether* silent, reply the advocates, there are many references to some kind of a shroud, which may or may not be the Shroud of Turin. At least these references prove the existence of a persistent tradition concerning the Shroud mentioned by the Evangelists. And there is the Iconographic Theory, which, speaking through the voice of art history, shatters the silence of those thousand years.

The charge of medieval forgery made by Bishop d'Arcis, however, remains to bedevil those who believe in the cloth. The tendency—justifiable to some extent—has been to by-pass it because of the favourable scientific evidence. But the angry Bishop of Troyes is still a stumbling block, although in reality it is not his opinion or even that of the anti-Pope Clement VII that counts. What matters is one paragraph in d'Arcis' 600-year-old letter:

> Eventually, after diligent inquiry and investigation, he discovered the fraud and how the said cloth had been cunningly painted, the truth being attested by the artist who had painted it, to wit, that it was a work of human skill, and not miraculously wrought or bestowed.

The import of those words, written by a high Catholic official, seems unmistakable. Yet, bafflingly, there is no sign of pigment in the threads of the cloth, nor any of the other obvious things that would point unerringly to the machination of some shadowy medieval painter. And what of the negativity and its perfection, inquire the relic's supporters? How explain the fact that the picture on the Shroud does not fit into the known history of the art of medieval times? Could an artist of such towering abilities have been unknown to his contemporaries? Why is there only this one example of his genius?

The Shroud and the d'Arcis letter are in direct conflict as they stand. So far, there has been no serious questioning of the authenticity of the Lirey documents, although everyone in the case has been eyed suspiciously. However, at least one explanation has been offered to resolve the difficulty, although its effect has been merely to widen the argument. The translation of the medieval Latin contained in the d'Arcis letter, Bulst contends, could just as well refer to a painter who *copied* the Shroud as to a painter who claimed to have executed it. He has also called attention to the unusual phrasing of the critical paragraph: " . . . it was a work of human skill and not miraculously wrought or bestowed." This seems more like the testimony of an "expert" witness, possibly one who had copied the Shroud and thought he had thereby proved its human origin. This kind of legal mentality was accepted in the Middle Ages. But here again, the problem has devolved into the never-never land of linguistic interpretation. Much more digging in the dusty archives of France will have to be done on the obscure personalities of Henry de Poitiers, Peter d'Arcis and Geoffrey de Charny before the full story of Lirey can be known.

An intriguing figure, this Geoffrey. The Shroud came into history through him, yet he never told where he got it, or if he told, it has remained a secret. The outlines of his own life are fairly well recorded. A soldier of renown, he was noted for personal bravery. Deeply religious, he was also a writer— there still exist three historical works by him, one in verse. He took part in the Crusade of 1346 against the Turks and was killed in the battle of Poitiers in 1356, after spending some time as a prisoner of the English. It is said that he died while trying to save King Philip from a lance-thrust. The spear that took his life also managed to cut in two the history of the Shroud. When the link between Geoffrey and the darkness beyond is finally restored, the Turin enigma will lose much of its mystery.

Ultimately, the truth about the relic will not be found through scripture or history, although both of these are indispensable controls. Only science can render a final verdict. If the relic is a forgery, science will detect it when given the chance; a hoax, supposedly perpetrated in the Middle Ages, could not continue to outwit modern techniques. Anthropology had to wrestle for forty years with the Piltdown fossil, before the chemical tests were developed that exposed it as an ingenious fraud. The Shroud of Turin is even more liable to exposure under searching inquiry than that famous forgery because of the large number of intricate and interrelated details it contains.

Since the end of the Second World War this inquiry— restricted to the photographs as it is—has continued with accelerated tempo. The early theories explaining the origins of the imprint, for instance, have been tested and retested, gradually undergoing refinement. Vignon's turn-of-the-century *vaporograph* idea has not completely satisfied some modern inquirers, who nevertheless believe in the cloth. They point out among other things, that ammonia vapours do not travel in straight lines but diffuse themselves. Vignon in his later years agreed that the chemical basis of the theory needed more study in the light of modern research. He suggested, for instance, that the ammonia vapours might have been held to an approximately straight-line movement by the humid atmosphere inside the Shroud.

Today, the exact secret of the imprints is still being sought by authorities such as Giovanni Judica-Cordiglia, Professor of Legal Medicine at the University of Milan. This scientist has, in addition, performed a complete anthropometric measurement on the body images, demonstrating their remarkable correspondence with reality.

The bloodstains on the wrist have been given a major share of attention. Their angle of flow has been plotted geometrically and in every instance the meanderings of the blood, even the smallest divergencies, agree with the laws of gravity and the contours of the arm. Pierre Barbet's work on the wound in the side received support from the experiments of Antoine Legrand, who demonstrated on a living body that the undulations of the flow from the lance wound matched the position and sequence of human ribs. No matter where scientists have turned in their probing for flaws or corroboration, they have been faced with this astonishingly consistent agreement with medical truth. Even the pronounced impression of the chest in the image, with the accompanying concavity of the abdomen, has been shown to agree with the effects of death by crucifixion.

Recognition of the importance of all these new developments was accorded by the *Catholic Encyclopedia*, which in 1957 published a revision of Father Thurston's forty-five-year-old article on the Shroud. In the *Supplement*, three full pages, with a page of illustration, now tell the story of sindonology with emphasis on the scientific details. Although the literature of both sides is listed, the article leans heavily towards authenticity. (See bibliography under *Abbott*.)

Though believers in the relic claim that the work already done, through the pictures, amply proves authenticity, they are anxious that the cloth itself should finally be submitted to direct testing. Resolutions to that effect were adopted at the 1939 convention and again at another congress in 1950. But the House of Savoy, in the person of its head, ex-King Umberto, has rejected the proposal (although the Italian monarchy was deposed in 1946, the Italian courts declared that the Shroud remains the exiled King's personal property). For some this attitude is incomprehensible at best, and at worst it points to a fear of what might be disclosed. The truth is, however, that this problem of physical testing is not a simple one. The Shroud is, after all, a spiritual object, hallowed by the prayers and devotion of many millions of pilgrims, and by the veneration of Popes and saints. Its true value is religious and, if it is authentic, it goes far beyond even such archaeological wonders as the Rosetta Stone or the clay tablets of Nineveh. Those who have inherited the task of safeguarding it and preserving it into the future feel their obligation heavily. They are understandably slow to endanger even the smallest fragment of it.

In the end, the question of direct testing will depend on just *how* the cloth is to be examined, Many tests have been proposed, but some of these would harm or destroy the material tested while others would not. About still others, there is uncertainty.

In the field of photography, colour and X-ray pictures would be made as a matter of course, without fear of damage. Other camera techniques have been perfected since Enrie made the last photos, such as microphotography, and these undoubtedly would be used. But photographic use of ultra-violet and infra-red rays might affect both the cloth and the imprint. Infra-red, for instance, generates a penetrating heat.

Spectrum analysis, which could probably identify the substances of the imprint and settle the question of the bloodstains, would likely have no bad effect, although this isn't sure. Direct chemical analysis of the blood, naturally, would mean the destruction of whatever samples were used and, according to some chemists, might even give uncertain results because of the age of the blood. It has been noted, though, that bloodstains from some Egyptian mummies have been analysed and even typed. Microscopic examination, especially with the modern miracle of the electron microscope, might yield decisive results.

Frequently called for is the radiocarbon method of dating organic objects. This test, supposedly, would settle the age of the cloth, but it can stand as a good example of the difficulties facing those who must make the decision to test, and those who must do the actual work.

Radiocarbon dating is a comparatively recent development, in practical use for little more than a decade, but it has already been hailed by archaeologists as an indispensable tool. Perfected by Dr. Willard Libby of the University of Chicago, it received wide public attention early in its career by helping to authenticate the Dead Sea Scrolls. (A portion of the linen found with the scrolls was tested by Libby and successfully dated between 167 B.C. and A.D. 233.)

But there are a number of drawbacks to this method, not the least of which is the destruction of the material to be dated. The procedure consists of burning the sample (in the case of the Shroud this would be almost the size of a handkerchief, more if confirmation tests were run), and reducing it to pure carbon. A gas counter then measures it in the form of carbon dioxide, methane or acetylene to determine its Carbon-14 content. The answer is given with a plus-or-minus factor, and with the shroud, this could vary anywhere from 100 to 400 years.

The real problem, however, is not the destruction of the material, but the fact that the shroud may not be suitable for radiocarbon dating. Contamination over the centuries could drastically alter and falsify the results. A number of experts have pointed out that the Shroud—which has not enjoyed the undisturbed, airless existence of the Dead Sea Scrolls— may have undergone an exchange of Carbon-14 between its own molecules and atmospheric dioxide. And, they say, there is also the possibility of contamination through microbiological action such as might arise in damp conditions. But research is still being done on the problem of sample reliability in radiocarbon dating and a usable technique may some day be evolved.

The Shroud of Turin has outlived its stormy past when men grew heated in defence or attack. The controversy is still there, but it is subdued, as if both sides are waiting for something they know is inevitable. Now, the relic reposes peacefully on silk cushions in the darkness of its silver casket. Every day men and women walk softly into the quiet chapel to stare for a few moments at the dim recess above the black marble altar. They kneel and cross themselves and pray. But often they wonder.

NOTES AND SOURCES

While this book is not intended as a scholarly work and so does not require extensive critical apparatus, some indication of the main sources from which I drew my facts may be pertinent. Mingled with these citations will be found some additional information on each chapter that I consider to be valuable or at least interesting.

CHAPTER ONE: The description of the inaugural ceremonies of 1898 is reconstructed from contemporary accounts in Turin newspapers, especially *Corriere Nazionale* and *La Stampa*, and from *La. S. Sindone che si venera a Torino* (1901) by Giammaria Sanno Solaro. The function was in reality more elaborate than I have shown it here; there were, for instance, missionary delegates from as far away as Egypt and China.

CHAPTER TWO: Giuseppe Pia of Turin was my main source for information about his father's life and work; he also gave permission to make use of his article in *Sindon* magazine for April, 1960 (*Sindon* is the official magazine, published quarterly, of the International Centre of Sindonology, with headquarters at Via San Domenico 28, Torino, Italy). This article, entitled "The First Photograph of the Holy Shroud," is a valuable document in the Shroud story since so few of the details were preserved at the time. Equally valuable is Secondo Pia's own *Memoria sulla riproduzione fotografica della santissima Sindone.* This is a short account of Pia's work on the night of May 28th, prepared in 1907 at the request of Arthur Loth, a French journalist. It appeared first in Loth's 1910 book, later in René Colson's *Le Portrait du Christ*, and was appended to the son's *Sindon* article. Pia's reaction to his first sight of the Holy Face is taken from this *Memoria*. Additional Pia background was obtained from "Comm. Avv. Secondo Pia," an obituary article by C. Parnisetti in the *Bulletin of the Royal Sub-Alpine Club* for January-June 1942. The original camera and photographic plate are still preserved at Turin, the first by the son, who kindly showed it to me, and the second at the newly-born museum of the Holy Shroud, where I was allowed to view it through the kindness of the director, Father Piero Coero-Borga. Throughout his life Pia continued to reap artistic and scholarly honours. As late as 1926 he was awarded a gold medal at an international builders exhibition. He also collaborated on a number of books, the most successful of which were *The Arch of Augustus at Susa* (1901), and a small volume about his native Asti. He died on September 7th, 1941 at the age of 86.

CHAPTER THREE: So far as I have been able to find, the picture was not published in any book or newspaper during 1898 or 1899. (By newspaper, I mean the special photo sections then common; news columns had not yet begun to include pictures.) There seem to have been at least two exceptions in the magazine field: a rather large reproduction in the Christmas 1898 supplement of the British *Photogram*; and the whole Shroud in positive (not the Pia negative) in *Arte Sacra* for late 1898. The first appearance between hard covers was probably in 1900 in Arthur Loth's *Le Portrait de N.S. Jesus Christ*. Loth, writer and later editor for *La Verité Français*, was one of the earliest champions of the Shroud outside Italy. He took an especially active part in publicizing the Delage report to the French Academy, described in Chapter 8. Sources in addition to those named in the text were: interview with Mr. Vittorio Marchis, son of one of the members of the committee that handled the dissemination of the picture, and the Guiseppe Pia article in *Sindon* (see Notes, Ch. 2). The story in *Osservatore Romano* on June 15th is signed "F.C." and is probably by the same Fillipo Crispolti who broke the news in *Il Cittadino*. Coverage by the American press is surprisingly sparse, but it was just at this time that we were building up to the initial invasion of Cuba during the Spanish-American War. Judging by the amount of news space given to these military events, the invasion seems to have been the only story that anyone then cared about.

CHAPTER FOUR: Purposely kept brief, this chapter is intended only as an outline of the historical discussion of the Shroud. It is a compound of the information contained in Wuenschel, *Self-Portrait of Christ*; Bulst, *The Shroud of Turin*; Beecher, *The Holy Shroud*; Pugno, *La Santa Sindone*; and Malijay, *Le Saint Suaire de Turin*. Two points I did not choose to treat in the text should be mentioned here. Beecher gives prominence to the visions of a certain St. Nino regarding the Shroud. A fourth-century Georgian princess, Nino is supposed to have revealed that the relic was taken from the tomb by St. Peter who kept it hidden for some time, but the reference has not attracted the attention of other Shroud advocates, except Barnes. Although Beecher cites his sources, their provenance seems very doubtful. The second point has long been a thorn in the side of Shroud supporters. It concerns a trial-by-ordeal to which the Shroud was supposedly submitted in the sixteenth century. Antoine de Lalaing, an ancient chronicler, contended that the relic, in 1503, was boiled in oil and then washed to test its authenticity—the idea being that if it were genuine it would be miraculously preserved. This statement has alternately puzzled and horrified believers and no one to date has known quite what to make of it. Some have rejected it as a pure legend, an interpolation or a mistranslation. It is the opinion of Father Wuenschel, told to me in Rome, that the incident never happened and that Lalaing was reporting it as something that supposedly took place long before his time. Regarding Geoffrey de Charny and his acquiring of the Shroud, there are only two contemporary clues, neither of which offers much information. A letter of the anti-Pope Clement VII to Geoffrey's son implies that Geoffrey himself claimed that it was given to him as a present. Eighty-seven years after Geoffrey's death, his granddaughter, Margaret de Charny, said it had been acquired as a spoil of war. Usually cited along with these two texts is another, originating at least 169 years after Geoffrey's death, that says he received the cloth from Philip of Valois, King of France, as a reward for his valour in battle. Historians have wrestled for years with these tantalizing possibilities without any marked success. Interesting is the fact that Geoffrey's son himself seems to have been uncertain about the Shroud's origins. In the controversy with d'Arcis he refers to it as "a likeness, i.e., a representation of the Shroud of Jesus." It is obvious that there are not enough facts available yet to permit safe conclusions. The Robert de Clari statement, concerning the Shroud seen in the Blachernes church at Constantinople in 1204, has caused a sub-controversy all its own. What exactly did the Old French word *figure* mean—"face" or "form?" Writers have translated it variously and there seems no way now of making sure just what de Clari saw, or claimed to have seen, on the Shroud of Constantinople. Even if the primary meaning of the word is "face" it would prove nothing, since de Clari might have been referring to only a part—the most striking part—of what he saw.

CHAPTER FIVE: Chevalier's background is based mainly on information found in a souvenir volume published by his friends in 1903: *Chevalier:*

Son Oeuvre Scientifique Sa Bio-bibliographie. Chevalier produced about a dozen writings on the subject between 1899-1903. The most important are: 1) *Le SS. de Turin est-il l'originale ou une copie?* Chambery, 1899, 31 pp.; 2) *Etude Critique sur l'origine du SS. de Lirey-Chambery Turin,* Paris, 1900, 59 pp. plus 60 pp. of documents; 3) *Le SS. de Turin et les defenseurs de son authenticite,* Paris, 1902, 45 pp.; 4) *Autour des origines du Suaire de Lirey avec documents inedits,* Paris, 1903, 53 pp. It is the opinion today that of the fifty or so documents cited by Chevalier regarding the affair at Lirey, only four have value as bearing directly on the point at issue, and of these only one stands up as an independent witness—the memorandum of d'Arcis. This is preserved in two examples at the Bibliotheque Nationale in Paris. One seems to be a draft, incomplete, and the other a copy, complete, both are unsigned and undated. The original is apparently not preserved and there is some question as to whether it was ever actually sent to Clement. Noguier de Malijay unhesitatingly brands the memorandum a forgery (*Bulletin du Saint Suaire No. 7*). The Lirey affair has such a tendency to create confusion that too often a prime fact is lost sight of: d'Arcis is the only source for the statement than an investigation was conducted and that a painter confessed. Even old histories of the Troyes diocese do not mention this. Confusion also exists as to the amount of credit due Chevalier for bringing the Lirey story to light. It has been pointed out, for instance, that a paper on the Lirey affair appeared in France in 1877, written by Canon Lalore, and was reprinted in 1888 (Loye), 1895 (*Melanges lit. dioc. de Troyes*), and 1899 (Prevost). Chevalier used Lalore's study as the basis of his own first two articles but openly acknowledged his debt (see page 124 *Etude Critique*). It is entirely possible that Chevalier was independently familiar with the Lirey story, perhaps even before Lalore's original publication. This would seem a point now beyond the possibility of settlement.

CHAPTER SIX: The facts of Paul Vignon's life were obtained from taped interviews with his family: M. and Mme. Jacques Vignon, Mme. René de Montuel and Vicomtesse Bernard de Lamotte. There is no personal data on him in print. That Vignon was the first to climb *l'Aiguille Meridionale d'Arves* is a tradition in his family, but an unofficial listing in an article in *Annuaire du Club Alpin Francais* for 1891 gives that honour to W. Coolidge. In any case, Vignon apparently thought himself the first. This same article, "The First Female Ascent of l'Aiguille Meridionale d'Arves," provided the description of the summit and its view. René Colson has always been a dim figure in the story of the Shroud and my own efforts produced very little information about him. He was born in 1853 at Nantes; entered the *Ecole Polytechnique* as a student in 1873, where he was a classmate of Henri Poincare, and later became a teacher there. In 1914 he produced a short book in support of the Shroud. He died about 1925. My keenest disappointment in research was a failure to locate any notebooks Vignon may have kept during his early work on the relic. According to Mme. de Montuel, all his papers were given to the *Institut Catholique*, but the archives there do not contain them. The archivist, Père Salles, informed me that the Nazis destroyed or took away a portion of the collection and left the rest in chaos. In reconstructing the details and sequence of Vignon's work I have relied almost exclusively on his own *The Shroud of Christ*. As a biologist, Vignon is known for his *Elements of Experimental Biology* (1931). Other works by him are: *Au Souffle de l'Esprit de la Creatur*, posthumously published in 1946, and *Le Saint Suaire de Turin* (1938) which is discussed in the notes to chap. 12.

CHAPTER SEVEN: This is also based on Vignon's *The Shroud of Christ*. Although he does not say so, Vignon knew he was entering a highly controverted field when he began looking into the biblical accounts of Christ's burial. Even apart from the Shroud, exegetes had long contended with each other over the provisional or definitive nature of the burial. Vignon cleared his theories and conclusions with theologians before announcing them. St. John's use of *othonia* and *sudarium* in referring to the grave cloths, constitutes the second phase of the "biblical difficulty." Opponents usually hold that neither of these words can be taken to mean a large piece of linen such as the Turin relic. However, arguments of equal force have been advanced by the Shroud's advocates to show that either *othonia* or *sudarium* could be equivalent to *sindon*, the word used by the Synoptics and about which there is no difficulty. It should be noted further, that in translating St. John, the words "wrapped up into one place," may also be rendered "*rolled* up into one place."

CHAPTER EIGHT: The room at the Academy where Delage gave his report is still in use. During a visit there I attended one of the regular Monday afternoon meetings and so have first-hand experience of the interminable *brouhaha* which continues to serve as background to all lectures. Today the the speaker does not stand beside the President's desk as did Delage, but in a special enclosure set against the opposite wall. The manuscript of the talk by Delage has been lost; at least a notation in the files of the Academy indicates that it was returned to "owner," but the families of neither Vignon nor Delage possess it. However, it was easily reconstructed from Delage's open letter in *Revue Scientifique* 4 ser. vol. 17 (1902) pp. 683-687, and the official report in *Comptes Rendus hebdomadaires des seances de l'Académie des sciences*, 134 (1902) pp. 902-904. The immediate occasion for Delage's open letter to the *Revue* is interesting. At the conclusion of his lecture on April 21, he gave his manuscript to the secretary, Pierre Berthelot, for inclusion in the *Comptes Rendus*. Berthelot, one of the leading rationalists of the day, printed only the part dealing with the chemical experiments; it appeared as an "extract" under the heading "On the formation of negative images by the action of certain vapours." It contained no mention of the Shroud. Delage considered this an arbitrary and bigoted action and drew up his letter, including the omitted portions of the lecture, for the *Revue*, the editor of which, Charles Richet, was a friend. Nowhere else in all the newspaper coverage is there any verbatim report of the talk. The best and most favourable reportage is that by Arthur Loth, who devoted seven lengthy stories in *La Verité Française* to the lecture and its aftermath in April, May and June. He also wrote a five-column, 4,000-word review of Vignon's book. My source for the length of time taken by the Academy to consider the proposal for intervention occurs in the *Comptes Rendus*, 134, p. 904. The report of the Belgian scientist—A. Vandevelde—is in *Comptes Rendus*, 134, pp. 1453-1454. This too was "extracted" by Berthelot and contains no mention of the Shroud. In 1903 Ulysse Chevalier alleged (in *Autour des Origines* etc.), that the Vatican's Congregation of Rites had privately condemned the relic in a report to Pope Leo XIII. The claim is still repeated today, but the fact seems to be that no such investigation was ever undertaken and Chevalier was too hasty in putting a rumour into print (see an article by Luigi Fossati in March 1960 *Sindon*). According to Father Wuenschel, this *faux-pas* by Chevalier earned him a private but official reprimand. Some of the attempts to answer Delage and Vignon scientifically deserve mention. De Mely charged that the image on the cloth had been stamped or printed on by means of wooden blocks. Other critics averred that the Shroud must have been reversed and that the actual painting was on the other side, the reversal probably having been done by the nuns who repaired the relic in 1534. This theory was not finally discarded until the discovery of a copy made in

1516 which showed the relic as it appears to day: wound on the right side, left hand crossed over the right, etc. Another suggestion was that the red lining on the back showed through. Since the photographs of 1931, all such claims have been forgotten. Main sources for the background of Delage were: taped interviews with a grandson, Professor Charles Deviller; a daughter, Mme. C. Deviller; and a daughter-in-law, Mme. Marcel Delage. I also made use of three pamphlets: *Yves Delage et son Oeuvre*, by Louis Boutan; Bordeaux, 1921; *Yves Delage*, a reprint by the Academy of Sciences of a discourse by Louis Joubin; and *Travaux de la Station Biologique de Roscoff*, by Charles Perez, Paris, 1926. Delage died in 1920 of uremic poisoning at the age of 66. He is buried at Sceaux, in the same cemetry that holds the body of Mme. Curie.

CHAPTER NINE: I have been able to find only two printed sources for the life of Thurston: a short biography, *Father Thurston*, by Joseph Crehan, S.J., London and New York, 1952; and an article in *The Month* for December, 1939, by John Murray, S.J. Between 1902 and 1930, Father Thurston wrote nine articles on the Shroud of Turin but one of these was in French and it was never translated. The substance of it, however, is contained in the other eight. (A complete listing will be found in the Bibliography. Beecher's writings are also listed there.) One of the puzzling things in the Thurston story is his lapse into silence after the new pictures became available in 1931. He took no part in the renewed discussion and wrote no more on the Shroud, although he continued to live and work for eight years thereafter. Crehan's biography of him makes no mention of his involvement with the relic, beyond a listing in the bibliography, though his career as a controversialist is well-covered. Father Crehan told me, at an interview in London, that the omission was dictated by the necessity of choosing from Thurston's voluminous output—a truly formidable task. He also told me that there was nothing among the Thurston papers that might indicate the drift of his opinion after 1931. According to a letter supposedly sent to Prof. Vittorio Ceroni of New York University in the late thirties, Thurston remained a sceptic to the end. The extracts in the text are from his two articles for *The Month* for January and February, 1903. The Beecher quote is from his 1928 book.

CHAPTER TEN: Giuseppe Enrie left a full description of his work in *La Santa Sindone Rivelata dalla Fotografia*, Turin, 1938. All the Turin newspapers carried circumstantial descriptions of the Exposition of 1931, but I have drawn especially on *Gazzetta del Popolo* for May 4th. For the results of the new photos I have consulted, in addition to Enrie, *La Santa Sindone nella costituzione tessile*, by Virginio Timossi, Turin, 1933; *L'Ostensione della S. Sindone*, Turin, 1931; and an article by A. S. Barnes in the *Dublin Review*, vol. 192 (1933), entitled "The New Evidence Concerning the Holy Shroud of Turin." I have also had recourse to both Wuenschel and Bulst (see Biblio.). The claim by the Shroud's adherents that fourteenth-century France did not know or use the twill weave has been met by the suggestion that the hypothetical forger might have purposely procured a piece of linen from the Orient. The retort is that such a subtle piece of skulduggery was completely foreign to the mentality of the Middle Ages.

CHAPTER ELEVEN: There is no printed source for the life of Pierre Barbet; all my facts came from an interview with his daughter, Mlle. Jeanne Barbet. The opening scene is based on her vivid recollection of the incident. Barbet's original accounts of his early experiments were published in the *Bulletin de la Societe de Saint Luc, Saint Come et Saint Damien*, for May 1933 and March 1934. Copies of both issues were kindly loaned to me by Mlle. Barbet. Indispensable was Barbet's own *A Doctor at Calvary* (trans. by the Earl of Wicklow) New York, 1953. This book is a compendium of Barbet's Shroud writings, including *The Corporal Passion of Jesus Christ*. Barbet's theory about the "water" noticed by St. John has been challenged by Dr. Anthony Sava of New York (*American Ecclesiastical Review*, 1958) and others. Dr. Sava inclines to the possibility that it was clear serum from a stratified, bloody effusion between the rib cage and the lung. Weithold (in Bulst) thinks it may have been a "transudation from the pleural sac." Dr. Robert Bucklin (*Linacre Quarterly*, 1958) believes the truth might be a combination of the Barbet and Sava hypotheses. All these men agree, however, that "water" and blood did actually flow from the side of Christ. Barbet's visit to the 1933 Exposition and the remark of Dr. Hovelacque are both recounted in *A Doctor at Calvary*. Regarding the immediate cause of death on the Cross, a number of alternate theories have been advanced including circulatory failure, heart rupture, etc. But the subject becomes an intricately technical one, mixed with theological speculation, and is not directly connected with the Shroud's authenticity. A lighter note was provided in my research by some examples of Barbet's annotation of detective stories, of which his

daughter still retains a large collection. On one page in *Lessinger Plays
Detective* his precise handwriting questions a distance of 300 metres for
glass shattered in an explosion. Barbet died on December 17th, 1961.

CHAPTER TWELVE: In 1938 Paul Vignon published his second book on the
Shroud: *Le Saint Suaire de Turin devant la science, l'archeologie, l'histoire,
l'iconographie, la logique.* In it he presents the total argument, up to that
time, in favour of the relic. Almost a third of the book is given over to an
exposition of his "Iconographic Theory," with more than fifty illustrations.
Arrangements for an English translation of this work were begun but never
completed. The two Sindonological Congresses were fully reported in *La
Santa Sindone nella ricerche moderne—1939* and the same title for 1950. The
best source, and the most recent, for a study of the biblical difficulty is the
pamphlet by the Rev. Edward Wuenschel: *The Shroud of Turin and the Burial
of Christ*, New York, 1954. Father Wuenschel, of course, is a believer and
argues powerfully in that direction, but his careful and scholarly work
contains all the necessary material and references for an understanding of the
disagreement. An account of the work of Judica-Cordiglia may be found in
his *La Sindone*, Padua, 1961. Information about radiocarbon dating and its use
in Shroud testing was obtained from the *Biblical Archaeologist Reader*, New
York, 1961; and an article in *Sindon*, December 1961, which reports the
opinions of some disinterested British scientists. In 1946 the relic was
privately exposed for the monks in the mountain-top monastery of Mon-
tevergine ,Italy. It had been sent there secretly when war threatened in 1939.
Before it was returned to Turin at the war's end, Cardinal Fossati permitted
an exhibition for the cloistered monks who would otherwise never see it.
A final explanation of the imprint on the Shroud is still the central problem
in Sindonology. Since Vignon's day, it has been approached from many
different angles. But it involves some highly technical chemistry and the
merely general reader should be aware that he is liable to find himself
beyond his depth. Good summary discussions of the problem can be found
in Bulst, pp. 73–76 and Barbet, pp. 37–40.

It should be noted here that for all serious study of the Shroud, copies of
the pictures made directly from the original Enrie plates are necessary. In
the smaller-scale, often badly printed reproductions in magazines and books,
much of the pertinent detail is lost.

BIBLIOGRAPHY
OF SHROUD LITERATURE
IN ENGLISH

The items listed or mentioned here comprise all the books and most of the pamphlets and articles on the Shroud of Turin in English. Scholarly works as well as those of a popular nature are represented and I have tried to indicate some that have importance in the present study of the question. For extensive bibliographies in all languages, see Bulst and Wuenschel, below.

Books and Pamphlets

Barbet, Pierre, *A Doctor at Calvary*, New York, 1953, 178 pp. (This is discussed in the Notes on Chapter 11.) Trans. from the French.

Barnes, Arthur, *The Holy Shroud of Turin*, London, 1934, 71 pp. (Now partially dated, this was the first book in English to appear after the new pictures of 1931 had reawakened interest in the relic.)

Beecher, P. A., *The Holy Shroud. A Reply to the Rev. Herbert Thurston, S.J.*, Dublin, 1928, 197 pp. (This is discussed in Chapter 9.)

Bulst, Werner, *The Shroud of Turin*, Milwaukee, 1957, 167 pp. (The most recent full-scale study. A balanced and readable book, the author has had the collaboration of experts in many fields. Concludes in favour of authenticity, but surveys both sides of the controversy. Contains nine pages of bibliography.) Trans. from the German.

Chalice, The, "A Photograph of Christ." The entire summer 1937 issue of this magazine was devoted to a "popular and yet very thought-provoking study of the Shroud problem." Monastery of the Precious Blood, Brooklyn.

Cheshire, Group Capt. G. L.; *Pilgrimage to the Shroud*, New York, 1956, 74 pp. (A straightforward account of a visit to Turin by a crippled Scottish child named Josie Woolam who was seeking a cure. She was allowed to hold the rolled-up Shroud in her lap. The incident happened in 1955 and the book was published a year later but no cure was reported.)

Frean, W., *The Winding Sheet of Christ*, Ballarat (Australia), 1960. 77 pp.

Fox, Langton, *The Holy Shroud*, London, 1956, 23 pp. (A Catholic Truth Society pamphlet favouring authenticity.)

Hynek, Rudolph, *Science and the Holy Shroud* (trans. from the Czech), 1936, 140 pp.

——, *The True Likeness* (trans. from the Czech), New York, 1951, 96 pp. (This author was one of the most active publicists of the Shroud of recent times; his works have been widely translated. However, he must be read with caution since his enthusiasm too often leads him to make unfounded claims and to present as fact what is only conjecture. For corrective comment on the serious and perplexing errors of Hynek, readers should consult Wuenschel's articles in *American Ecclesiastical Review* for 1953, see below.)

McEvoy, W., *The Death-image of Christ*, Melbourne, 1945, 96 pp.

O'Connell, P., *New Light on the Passion of Our Divine Lord*, Dublin, 1955. 86 pp.

Proszymski, Kazimir de., *The Authentic Photograph of Christ*, London, 1932. (A popularization of the new Enrie photos of 1931.)

Rinaldi, Peter, *I Saw the Holy Shroud*, Tampa, 1940, 67 pp. (A lucid presentation of the facts by a priest who acted as an interpreter at a special scientific conclave during the Exposition of 1933. Contains a question-and-answer section. The author is now pastor of Corpus Christi Church in Portchester, New York, where he has set up the only major shrine to the relic in the U.S. It is built around a life-size transparency of the frontal image on the Shroud.)

Vignon, Paul, *The Shroud of Christ* (trnas. from the French', New York and London, 1902, 170 pp. (This is discussed in the text.)

Weyland, Peter, *A Sculptor Interprets the Holy Shroud*, Esopus, New York, 1954, 32 pp. (The author describes his studies in modelling a corpus after the details on the cloth.)

Wuenschel, Edward, *Self-Portrait of Christ*, Esopus, New York, 1954, 126 pp. (This work remains the best introduction to the subject for serious readers. Contains 19 pages of bibliography.

——, *The Holy Shroud of Turin*. This occupied an entire issue of *Perpetual Help* magazine, vol. XIII, pp. 97-144, 1950. Condensed in *The Catholic Digest*, XIV, 1950, pp. 77-83.

Wuenschel Edward, *The Shroud of Turin and the Burial of Christ*, Esopus, New York, 1954, 84 pp. (A deep study, complete with critical citations, of the biblical difficulty. It originally appeared as two articles in *The Catholic Biblical Quarterly* for October 1945 and April 1946.)

Articles

Abbott, Walter, "The Shroud and the Holy Face," *American Ecclesiastical Review*, CXXXII (1955), pp. 239-263. (A survey of Shroud studies at the time of writing.)

——, "Did Christ Leave a Picture of Himself in the Shroud of Turin?" *The Pilot* (Boston), April 17, 1954, p. 9. Reprinted in *The Catholic Mind*, November, 1954.

——, "Shroud, The Holy," *Catholic Encyclopedia*, Supplement II, Seventh Section, vol. XVII (1957). (This is a corrective to the wholly condemnatory 1912 article by Father Thurston.)

Action magazine, "The Holy Shroud of Turin," vol. 1, no. 8 (November 1938), pp. 4-9.

Ashe, Geoffrey, "The Holy Shroud of Turin," *The Sunday Express*, March 25, 1962.

Barclay, Vera, "The Shroud is More than a Relic," *Pax, The Quarterly Review of the Benedictines of Prinknash* (England), Spring 1958, pp. 10–15 (On Paul Claudel's writings on the Shroud).

——, "Radioactive Carbon Dating for the Holy Shroud," *Sindon*, December 1961, pp. 35–37. (Report on views of some British physicists on the problems involved.)

Barnes, Arthur, "What is the Holy Shroud? A Reply to Fr. Thurston, S.J." *The Universe*, April 7, 1930 (Critical of Thurston's 1912 Cath. Ency. article).

——, "The Holy Shroud of Turin," *Catholic Medical Guardian*, July, 1930.

——, "The New Evidence Concerning the Holy Shroud," *Dublin Review*, January 1933, pp. 26–42. (Based on the pictures taken in 1931, this was the second serious attempt to break through the long period of silence that followed Thurston's early rejection of the relic.)

Beecher, P. A., "The Holy Shroud of Turin," *Irish Ecclesiastical Record*, ser. 5, vol. 25, pp. 49-66.

Beecher, P. A., "The Holy Shroud from the Artistic Viewpoint," *Irish Ecclesiastical Record*, ser. 5, vol. 24, pp. 461-475.

——, "The Crucifixion as Told in the Holy Shroud," *Irish Ecclesiastical Record*, ser. 5, vol. 55, pp. 582-590.

Belam, O. H., "The Holy Shroud of Turin—A Doctor's Meditation," *Catholic Medical Quarterly*, October, 1959, pp. 113-126 (Favourable to authenticity).

Bucklin, Robert, "The Medical Aspects of the Crucifixion," *Linacre Quarterly*, February 1958. (A version of this was presented at the International Congress of Legal and Social Medicine in Vienna, May 1961, and was later printed in *Sindon*, December 1961.)

Cheshire, Group Capt. G. L., "How Christ Was Crucified," *Picture Post*, April 9, 1955, pp. 11-17.

Chevalier, Ulysse, "The Holy Shroud and the New Testament" (trans. from the French by Fr. Joseph Flynn), *The Pilot* (Boston), November 8, 1902.

Evening Journal (New York), "The Modern Miracle of Christ's Winding Sheet That Has Stirred Up All Europe," Sunday Magazine, May 26, 1898, p. 15. (The same paper for late 1933 carried a full-page, illustrated, article on the relic. I was shown a copy of it in Turin but there was no date. Efforts to trace the exact reference in New York libraries were unavailing.)

Houédard, Silvester, "Do We Know What Our Lord Looked Like? Recent Research on the Holy Shroud," *Pax*, *The Quarterly Review of the Benedictines of Prinknash* (England), Autumn 1957.

Illustrated Magazine, "Do We Possess Christ's Photograph," (trans. from the French by R. Crawford), London, vol. 27, 1902, pp. 291-305.

Kennedy, T. R., "The Holy Shroud—An Unusual Relationship Between Faith and Science," *The Bulletin of the Philosophy and Science Group*, Newman, Association (England), May 1956.

Kenyon, Sir F., "The Case for the Holy Shroud," *Discovery*, vol. 15 (1934), pp. 121-123.

Lancet, The, "The Winding Sheet of Christ," April 26, 1902, p. 1216. Also, "Does the Dead Body Possess Properties Akin to Radioactivity?" same vol. p. 1201.

Mackey, H. B., "The Holy Shroud of Turin," *Dublin Review*, CXXXII (1903), pp. 1-33.

McNasby, Clement, "The Holy Shroud and Art," *Catholic Biblical Quarterly*, April 1945. (An interesting study of the relic from the viewpoint of the history of art.'

Meldola, R., (Untitled) *Nature Magazine*, vol. 67 (1903), pp. 241-243. (A highly unfavourable review of Vignon's 1902 book.)

Nature Magazine, "M. Vignon's Researches and the Holy Shroud," vol. 66 (1902), pp. 13-14.

O'Gorman, P. W., "The Holy Shroud of Christ. Reply to Arguments Against Its Authenticity," *The Irish Catholic*, December 18, 1941 and January 1, 1942.

——, "The Holy Shroud of Jesus Christ. New Discovery of the Cause of the Imprints," *American Ecclesiastical Review*, CII (1940) pp. 208-226. (Concerns the possible action of radioactivity in the formation of the imprint, an idea now rejected.)

O'Rahilly, Alfred, "Jewish Burial," *Irish Ecclesiastical Record*, LVIII (1940) pp. 123-135.

——, "The Burial of Christ," *Irish Ecclesiastical Record*, LVIII (1940) pp. 302-316; 493-503; LIX (1941) pp. 150-171.

Otterbein, Adam, "And immediately there came out blood and water," *Bulletin*, Holy Shroud Guild, vol. 7 (1958) no. 2.

Photogram, The, August 1898. A Report, quoting the *Daily Telegraph*, of first reactions in Turin to Pia's photographic discovery. Also, Christmas number *Supplement*. Contains what is probably the first magazine printing of the Pia negative.

Rengers, Christopher, "Shroud of Turin," *Extension*, July 1958, pp. 17, 30, 36.

Rinaldi, Peter, "The Holy Shroud," *Sign Magazine*, June 1934.

Sava, Anthony, "The Wounds of Christ," *Catholic Biblical Quarterly*, XVI (1954) pp. 438-443.

——, "The Blood and Water from the Side of Christ," *American Ecclesiastical Review*, CXXXVIII (1958) pp. 341-345.

——, "The Wound in the Side of Christ," *Catholic Biblical Quarterly*, XIX (1957) pp. 343-346.

Scientific American, vol. 86 (1902) verbatim reprint from *Nature*, vol. 66 (1902) pp. 13-14 (above).

Thurston, Herbert, "The Holy Shroud and the Verdict of History," *The Month*, CI (1903) pp. 17-29.

Thurston, Herbert, "The Holy Shroud as a Scientific Problem," *The Month*, CI (1903) pp. 162-178. (This item and the one above contain the authors' complete argument against the Shroud. The rest repeat the substance of these two, while adding incidental details.)

——, "The Holy Shroud of Turin," *The Tablet*, CI (1903) pp. 284-285.

——, "Shroud, The Holy," *Catholic Encyclopedia*, XIII (1912) pp. 762-763.

——, "The Holy Shroud," *The Month*, CX (1912) pp. 537-539.

——, "The Problem of the Holy Shroud," *Irish Ecclesiastical Record*, XXIV (1924) pp. 621-631.

——, "What in Truth Was the Holy Shroud?" *The Month*, CLV (1930) pp. 160-164.

——, "Relics Authentic and Spurious," *The Month*, CLVI (1930) pp. 51-63.

Time Magazine, May 15, 1950. A report on the Sindonological Congress then in progress at Rome. (The accompanying illustration is incorrectly printed.)

Vignon, Paul, and Wuenschel, Edward, "The Problem of the Holy Shroud," *Scientific American*, XCIII (1937) pp. 162-164. Condensed in *Reader's Digest*, XXX (1937) pp. 97-99.

Wuenschel, Edward, "The Photograph of Christ," *Pax*, XV (1937) pp. 112-115.

——, "The Holy Shroud. Present State of the Question," *American Ecclesiastical Review*, CII (1940) pp. 465-486.

——, "The Holy Shroud and Art," *Liturgical Arts*, IX (1941) pp. 29-36.

——, "The Truth about the Holy Shroud," *American Ecclesiastical Review*, CXXIX (1953) pp. 3-19, 100-114, 170-187. (A frank analysis of the extravagant errors in the work of Hynek.)

——, "Photograph of Christ," *Liguorian*, March and April 1963.

FOR THE RECORD

In the research and writing I have received valuable co-operation and many kindnesses from a number of people, and would like all of this to be part of the record.

It was in the 1954 book, *Self-Portrait of Christ*, by the Rev. Edward A. Wuenschel, C.SS.R., that I first found the idea from which the present work developed. Subsequently, in Rome and Turin, Father Wuenschel placed himself at my disposal, opening many doors and sharing with me many hours of conversation on the Shroud, a subject that has engrossed his attention for over a quarter of a century.* I am also indebted to Father Wuenschel's confrère, the Rev. Adam J. Otterbein, CSSR., President of the Holy Shroud Guild, Esopus, N.Y., for welcoming me into a field in which I had no official standing, and making his knowledge available to me without restrictions. Similarly, I was fortunate in making early contact with the Rev. Peter M. Rinaldi, S.D.B., Pastor of Corpus Christi Church, Port Chester, New York, whose thirty-year interest in the relic smoothed my initial probes. Perhaps my greatest debt is owed to W. Clement Stone, President of the Combined Insurance Company of America, Chicago, whose financial assistance made the entire project possible. A man of a thousand interests, Clem Stone is neither a Catholic nor an advocate of the Shroud, but his inquiring mind responded with enthusiasm to the challenge of the relic.

In Turin, the Rev. Piero Coero-Borga, Director of the Church of the Holy Shroud, the Rev. Luigi Fossati, of the Richelmy Institute, and the staff of the *Biblioteche Civiche* made my work easier. Giuseppe Pia, a busy city official of Turin, graciously made time to talk with me about his father and supplied me with copies of certain materials. Vittorio Marchis, of Turin, also shared with me his knowledge of the early excitement generated by Secondo Pia's picture, and Count Luigi Lovera di Maria talked with me of the work of his friend, Guiseppe Enrie. I was especially pleased by the interest in this work expressed by His Eminence, Maurillio Cardinal Fossati, of Turin.

*It is with great regret that I record the death of Fr. Wuenschel at Rome on January 6th, 1964. He leaves behind a large body of original research, on the historical aspects of the relic, on which he had been gathering for a definitive work.

In France, my efforts to locate relatives of Yves Delage were facilitated by the staff of the Archives of the Academy of Sciences. It was through the kind offices of Professor Charles Deviller, of the Sorbonne, a grandson of Delage, that I was finally enabled to talk with Delage's daughter, Mme. C. Deviller, and his daughter-in-law, Mme. Marcel Delage. Both ladies, now in their eighties, spoke of their illustrious relative with ready remembrance and a touching regard. The family of Paul Vignon extended welcome hospitality both in Paris and at their ancient *chateaux* in Rueil la Gadeliere. Present at these interviews were Jeanne de Montuel, a daughter of Vignon who mirrors the enthusiastic and helpful personality so often attributed to her father; Jacques Vignon, a son, with his wife B. Vignon, both of whom remained patient and understanding in the face of my incessant questioning; and Viscomtesse B. de Lamotte, a granddaughter who received her earliest lessons at the knees of the scientist and was with him at the end. Also present as somewhat puzzled spectators were the two daughters of Vtesse. de Lamotte: Laurence, age 8, and Dominique, age 6. In place of reminiscences of her great-grandfather, Dominique offered a rendition of *Frère Jacques*. For information about Dr. Barbet, I am indebted to his daughter Jeanne Barbet, who made herself and her home in Angers available to my questions and tape recorder for an entire day, providing full answers with rare insight into my objectives.

Also in France, I received timely assistance from the following: Père F. Salles, of the *Institut Catholique*; M. F. Beauchesne, of *Beauchesne et ses fils*, and Monique Cadic, of the same company. Maureen Docherty, of the *Alliance Française*, smoothed my unending questioning with her facile command of French. I am also grateful to the Rev. Joseph Crehan, S.J., of London, for the time he gave in discussing Father Thurston with me.

For help in the translation of Italian and French sources my thanks go to Conway Associates of New York; Marie Prochilo, of Port Chester, New York; the Rev. Raymond Turro, of Darlington, New Jersey. For critical readings of the manuscript, I thank Fathers Otterbein and Rinaldi and the Rev. James Galvin of Esopus. Early and welcome encouragement came from Kay Sullivan, Features Editor, *The Catholic Digest;* Paul Lapolla and Bertha Krantz of Random House; Evelyn Singer, of New York; and my wife, Dorothy, who also provided a running critical appraisal of the manuscript. A very special debt, for long-time encouragement, is owed to my mother.

INDEX